Resources for
Junior Highs in the Church

EXPLORE volume 2

James E. Grant, editor

JUDSON PRESS • VALLEY FORGE

EXPLORE, VOLUME 2

Copyright © 1976
Judson Press, Valley Forge, PA 19481

Unless otherwise indicated, Bible quotations in this volume are in accordance with the Revised Standard Version of the Bible, copyrighted 1952 and 1971 by the Division of Christian Education of the National Council of the Churches of Christ in the United States of America, and are used by permission.

Library of Congress Cataloging in Publication Data (Revised)

Main entry under title:

Explore—resources for junior highs in the Church.

    Vol. 2 edited by J. E. Grant
    Includes bibliography.
    1. Church work with children.   2. Children—Religious life.
I. Corbett, Janice M., ed.   II. Grant, J. E., ed.   III. Title.
BV639.C4C66   268'.433   74-8574
ISBN 0-8170-0720-2

Printed in the U.S.A.

Photo Credits: p. 22, Alan Cliburn; p. 50, H. Armstrong Roberts; p. 81, Clark and Clark; p. 94, David Strickler; p. 122, Bob Combs.

READ THIS
BEFORE YOU USE THIS BOOK

EXPLORE, Volume 2, is a RESOURCE book.

This means:

- You don't have to use everything in the book.
- You don't have to follow the order of the book.
- You can pick and choose, change and adapt.
- You can make the book *work for you*, rather than make yourself *work for the book*.

EXPLORE, 2, IS A TOOL FOR JUNIOR HIGH MINISTRY

Pick it up . . . get the "feel" of it . . . use it to mold a ministry that has meaning for YOUR GROUP.

To use *EXPLORE, 2*, follow these steps:

1. Read the LEADERSHIP SECTION first. This tells you what your job may be as you work with junior highs in your church.

2. Call together a planning group of junior highs. Let them look through *EXPLORE, 2*, to find some subjects that interest them.

3. Point out that *EXPLORE, 2*, has resources for:

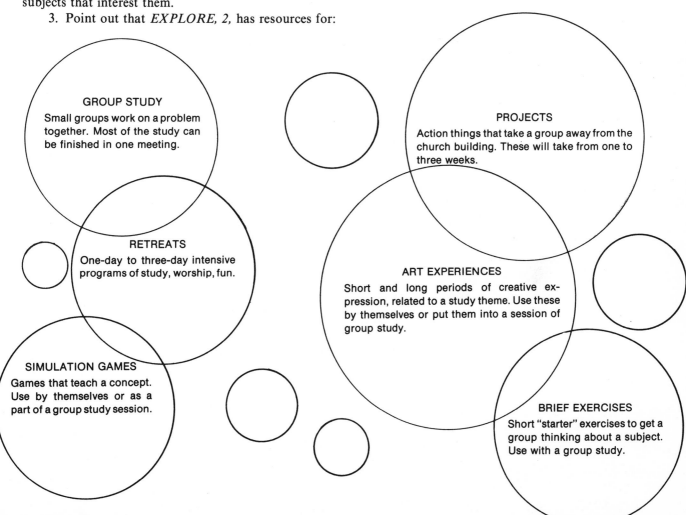

GROUP STUDY
Small groups work on a problem together. Most of the study can be finished in one meeting.

PROJECTS
Action things that take a group away from the church building. These will take from one to three weeks.

RETREATS
One-day to three-day intensive programs of study, worship, fun.

ART EXPERIENCES
Short and long periods of creative expression, related to a study theme. Use these by themselves or put them into a session of group study.

SIMULATION GAMES
Games that teach a concept. Use by themselves or as a part of a group study session.

BRIEF EXERCISES
Short "starter" exercises to get a group thinking about a subject. Use with a group study.

4. Decide what type of resource your group wants to use.

5. TRY IT. Then, when finished, EVALUATE IT. Find out what went wrong—and right. Use your experience to plan a better experience next time.

6. Turn to the WORSHIP section for worship suggestions.

7. For recreation suggestions, turn to the REC-REATION section.

8. Find more resources for junior high ministry in the ADDITIONAL RESOURCES section.

A SPECIAL NOTE

EXPLORE, Volume 2, has been written by many people who work with junior highs in churches. Their names are given at the end of each article. Special thanks to them and to the planning committee who dreamed up this volume: Donna Cullen, Jim Grant, Kenneth Hardy, Kenneth Ostermiller, Ronald Newsom.

—THE EXPLORE PEOPLE

CONTENTS

SECTION I
PROGRAM RESOURCES

SECTION I
Program Resources
About Faith

GROUP STUDY

RETREAT

PROJECTS

SHARPENING BIBLE STUDY SKILLS

Some tools for using the Bible

by JOHN L. ANDRES

WHY?

The Bible is the guide for Christians. We study the Bible to learn about our beginnings, to receive encouragement in our attempts to live the Christian life, and to find God's message for today. Developing Bible study skills is one of the most important tasks of a Christian.

Bible study skills can be sharpened primarily through *doing*. These study outlines will help youth *do* Bible study better. At the end of each session, have youth identify the skills they used in the study. The following is a partial list of those skills: (1) gaining the ability to understand the text; (2) asking the appropriate questions, such as why was this passage written? to whom? by whom? what does it say to me?; (3) learning where to find answers to these questions; (4) learning how to use resources effectively; (5) finding an approach to Bible study that is interesting; (6) learning how to use what the Bible says and applying it to our lives. Have those in the youth group compile their own list.

GOAL

To acquaint members with key resources to be used in Bible Study.

SUPPLIES NEEDED

Concordances, Bible dictionaries, at least two Bible commentaries, a Bible atlas, several Bibles, paper, and pencils.

PROCEDURE

Step 1

Hand out the Bible study resources (listed above),
making sure each member has at least one resource. If resources are limited, each of the members of the group should have at least a Bible. Select a word, such as "anger." Give the group ten minutes to discover as much as possible about what the Bible says about "anger." When the time is up, ask each person to share what he or she has discovered. How did the resource each was using help? Which resource was the most valuable in studying the biblical meaning of a word? (Some students will recognize right away that some resources, such as an atlas, are of little value in this exercise.)

Step 2

Have the group exchange resources. Be sure those who were using Bibles have a chance to use a resource. Have the group discover as much as possible about the book of Galatians. Limit the time to ten minutes. Again have participants report what they discovered and discuss the questions in Step 1.

Step 3

Exchange resources one more time. Have them look up James 2:26 and answer these questions: What did the author mean by this statement? Is this thought found anyplace else in the Bible? Follow the discussion procedure in Step 1.

Step 4

Personal Bible study provides much of the strength for many Christians' faith. It encourages them as they act out their faith. Ideally it gives persons a feeling of closeness to God. Beyond that, Bible study should propel us into *acting*. The following are some ways personal Bible study can be approached: (1) Follow a theme, such as "The Kingdom of God." (2) Study a word, such as "love." (3) Study a book of the Bible.

9

Include the history of the book, the authorship, the purpose of the book, and controversies regarding the book. (4) Study a personality, such as Paul, Peter, or Luke. Ask the group to add to the list.

Step 5

It is equally important to gather with friends to study the Bible together. This may be done in the youth group, a mixed group of youth and adults, or with a few school friends. By considering others' opinions, a person will grow in his or her own understanding of the Scripture. While methods of Bible study may be similar to those mentioned above for personal study, the individual has the added advantage of the group's supportive presence. Discuss briefly: could Bible study have a place in my life? What might we do as a group to sharpen our own Bible study skills?

IF YOU HAVE MORE TIME

A group with more time might want to sharpen its Bible study skills by studying the life and work of Paul. You will need a Bible commentary, a map of Paul's journeys, a Bible dictionary, *Halley's Bible Handbook*, other books that have information on Paul, poster board and felt-tip markers, or a 4' x 8' sheet of plaster board and tempera paint and brushes, rulers, pencils, and erasers.

Step 1

Introduce the man Paul to the group. *Halley's Bible Handbook* will provide some brief information on Paul. If possible, tell about Paul instead of reading from a book.

Step 2

Look at a map of Paul's journeys. Have the group discover the answers to the following questions by using Bible commentaries, Bible dictionaries, and books written about Paul: (1) How much distance did Paul travel on his journeys? (2) How did he travel? (3) How long did it take him to make each journey?

Step 3

Make a map. The map may be made in two ways: (1) using poster board and felt-tip markers; (2) using heavy plaster board and tempera paint. An average group might want to use the first alternative although the second alternative can be more fun and contain more learning opportunities. The outline of the map could be made in advance on the poster board to save time. It does not have to be exact in its dimensions. Locate and name the cities that Paul visited.

Have the members of the group take turns drawing a line from one of Paul's stops to the next stop. After the line is drawn, have another member read the Scripture passage about that particular stop. Be sure to note and discuss briefly the interesting people Paul met. Have any of the group met similar people? How does it *feel* to deal with people who resist you? Who support you? The group may move through this rapidly or stop and do further research. Have the resources available if further research is desired. The group may select only the most interesting of Paul's stops to study, or they may briefly study each stop. This should be adjusted to your particular group and its interest level.

A group that is willing to spend more time and is enthusiastic about Bible study might select the second way to make the map. Making a map on plaster board is more difficult as it should be scaled out to the right size and then painted in various colors to mark the countries. This map can be used later to do a program for church school classes. A total church worship service could be built as a result of the group's study and work. A map of this size could also be used for a display in the church.

Another possibility while making a map would be to make a slide show depicting Paul's journeys step by step. As the group marks the journey on the map, take slides of it. This makes it possible for the group to do a program showing the slides. As the journey progresses, persons might take turns explaining what happened. Giving a program gives the junior highs the opportunity to be educators of adults.

Step 4

In concluding your study, you might use the following questions either for silent reflection or for a short discussion: (1) Through a study of Paul we find he took his faith seriously. What might I do if I took my faith seriously? Would I do anything differently than I am now doing? If so, what changes or additions in action would I make in my life? (2) Paul had help on his journeys. What might our youth group do to help one another in acting out our own Christian faith? (3) Is there any similarity between Paul's journeys and our own journey through life?

Rev. John L. Andres is minister of the Exodus House Church in Jacksonville, Illinois.

WHICH TRANSLATION OF THE BIBLE FITS ME?

Choosing a personal Bible translation

by JOHN L. ANDRES

WHY?

Junior high youth sometimes have difficulty understanding the different translations and paraphrases of the Bible. Selecting a Bible for their own use can be very confusing. This program is designed to acquaint them with a number of biblical translations and paraphrases.

Because the Bible was originally written in Hebrew and Greek, scholars have had to translate the original biblical writings into other languages. Some common English translations are the King James Version, the Revised Standard Version, *The New English Bible,* and *The New Jerusalem Bible.* Others have paraphrased the English translations, that is, rewritten them in language that is more easily understood— often colloquial. Two common paraphrases are *The Living Bible* and the Cotton Patch Version of books of the New Testament.

For interesting background information read the preface of each Bible. This will give you a brief history of how the translation or paraphase came into being.

GOAL

To help the individual consider what is important in selecting a translation or paraphrase of the Bible for personal use.

PREPARATION

Gather as many translations and paraphrases of the Bible as possible. Your minister or church library will have these available. Have newsprint or chalkboard, paper and pencils on hand.

PROCEDURE

Step 1

Put all in the group at ease by letting them know they will not be tested on their knowledge of the Bible. If this program is going to help junior highs, it will require honesty on their part. You can set the pace by being honest yourself. That may be threatening, but it will pay off in honesty from the group.

WHY?

The Bible contains a vast amount of information. Even the best Bible students can be made to feel anxious if they believe they will be put on the spot. Groups tend to discuss the Bible on a superficial, safe level. This may be fun, but it may also be forgotten soon. Before junior highs will take seriously the selection of a translation, they need to be serious about their feelings regarding Bible study.

Step 2

Ask the group to write the word that first comes to mind when you say the following words: Bible, Old Testament, New Testament, study. List their reactions on newsprint. Do the words reflect positive or negative feelings? Give group members opportunities to share why they have particular feelings. It is important for the leader to allow expression of negative feelings if they are present. After the discussion share your own feelings about Bible study and what kind of experiences you have had. Do not dwell long at any point but still allow time for everyone who wishes to participate to do so.

Step 3

Divide the group into twos. Have them list what is important in selecting a Bible. Limit the time to ten minutes. Keep the process moving. On newsprint or chalkboard list what they believe to be important. Some things that might be included are: the ability to understand what is read, the availability of that Bible, the purpose of study, ease in using, Bible helps, theological consistency, and sentimental value.

Step 4

Have each person rank items on the list from the most important to the least important item. Next, have the members share their list with one other person. Then ask each person to share with the total group the first item on his or her list. Through this process the junior highs should begin to put in perspective the items they feel are important to have in their own personal Bible.

Step 5

Pass the translations and paraphrases of the Bible to the group. Look up 1 Corinthians 13:1-3. Have the members take turns reading the passage. List the differences on newsprint. Are there different meanings in the various Bibles? Which Bibles were the easiest to understand?

Step 6

Let persons in the group look at the various translations and paraphrases. Have them compare the Bibles with their list of criteria. Let them select the one they will use in future Bible study.

IF YOU HAVE MORE TIME

Researching the impact the various translations have had on the church might be very interesting. One such study would reveal how Wycliffe's attempt to translate the Bible into English resulted in his execution, and yet the King James Version was later based upon his work. Why was one attempt at translation acceptable and the other rejected as blasphemy? What happened in the church between the time of Wycliffe and King James?

Another project could be a short drama which would consist of each youth portraying a translation or paraphrase as the main character tries to select a Bible for his or her own use. The information for the skit could be taken from the prefaces of each Bible to be used. The skit should be written by the group around the translations and paraphrases they have available to use. It could include historical notes as well as the things the group feels are important considerations for selecting a Bible. Following is a brief skit to give you an idea of how it might be done.

WHICH ONE?

THE SCENE: A junior high youth is wandering about near the display of Bibles at a local store. She is trying to select a Bible from the many translations and paraphrases which are offered. Suddenly the following conversation takes place.

KING JAMES VERSION: Hey, wait a minute! Why did you put me back on the shelf? Aren't you going to buy me?

CINDY: I must be hearing things! Bibles don't talk!

KJV: Yes, we do! Usually people only listen to us while they are reading, but we do talk and communicate! But that's beside the point. Why aren't you going to buy me?

CINDY: Well, suppose you give me a good reason why I should?

KJV: I have a long history and an interesting one at that, I might say! I was published in 1611 in England after forty-seven men spent seven years working on me. Some of my passages were revised seventeen times before the committee would accept them. I lived two and one-half centuries before another version was made.

REVISED STANDARD VERSION: Just because you have been around so long doesn't make you the best! Cindy, you should consider me! I'm much more current than the King James Version. I was published in 1952 after thirty-two scholars worked for fifteen years. My pages consider all of the newly discovered material, and I've been written in a more modern vocabulary.

NEW ENGLISH BIBLE: Cindy, don't listen to them. I'm even more "with it" than they are. I was published in 1961. I'm much easier to read and understand, plus my texts are accurate. I'm the newest out!

CINDY: Oh, dear, I'm really confused now! Your

histories are interesting, but they don't help me decide which one of you is best for me. Oh, how will I ever decide! And there are so many more Bibles to look at. I guess I just won't buy one today. Maybe I can decide at a later time, but I'm just too confused right now.

KJV: Hey, wait a minute! Since I started this, I'd like to try to help. I guess I was just being a little selfish, but maybe I can help you. One of the most important things to remember in selecting one of us is that you need to love us. Then you will read our pages and put us to good use.

RSV: Yes, that's right. And in order to do that, you must be able to understand what you are reading. Each one of us is different in some ways, but only you can decide if we are easy for you to understand.

NEB: I have an idea! Why don't you take each one of us and look up the same passage of Scripture—one you aren't familiar with? Then see which one of us is easier for you to understand. Try this several times, and maybe it will help you decide.

Cindy: That's a good idea! Maybe it won't be too hard, after all.

KJV: Remember, look at the Bible helps, too. We have many different things, such as maps, cross references, concordances, red lettering of Christ's words, footnotes, etc. What you want depends upon individual preferences.

RSV: That's right, and remember there is nothing wrong with selecting one of us because of sentimental reasons.

NEB: The important thing to remember is to use whichever one of us you select. We can only help you grow if you talk with us.

CINDY: Thank you. You have really been very kind. I'm kind of excited about studying now.

Rev. John L. Andres is minister of the Exodus House Church in Jacksonville, Illinois.

WHY DENOMINATIONS?

Some common ground and differences between denominations

by LON SCHNEIDER

GOAL

To explore some of the differences in our many church denominations, to see some of our common ground and the need for unity to carry out the ministry of Christ.

WHY?

This is a broad topic on which one can easily spend many different sessions. The objective of this outline is only to scratch the surface. There are some suggested ideas for more depth if your group is interested in going deeper. Also at the end of the program outline are some specific suggestions for developing some future sessions should you like to look further at the many denominations making up the church of Jesus Christ.

GETTING STARTED

Have a sheet of newsprint or a chalkboard in the front of the group. Ask the youth to name their favorite television programs. Allow them to explain their choice in a sentence or two, but don't let others in the group discuss these selections. On the sheet of newsprint or chalkboard make a listing of all the programs that are mentioned.

After all have named their selections, you should have a listing of several programs with a wide range of reasons for the choices. Ask the group, "Why don't we all like the same program?" As you discuss this, you should be able to draw the conclusion that not everyone is alike and their tastes in life are going to be different.

Conclude this section by asking the young people to name the many church denominations with which they are acquainted. Make a similar listing of denominations on newsprint.

LOOKING AT DIVERSITY

One need only look at the "church page" in any newspaper to discover that not all churches are the same. Some have Masses while others have worship services; still others have reading services. Some will have church schools, and others won't. The approach to this section will depend upon your knowledge of church history and the maturity of the group. Approach A is an easier approach and requires little previous knowledge of other denominations. Approach B requires more knowledge on your part as a leader and more involvement in the discussion by the group of young people.

Approach A

Begin by telling the group of an experience you have had in worshiping in a church of another denomination. Tell of the differences you noticed. Was it a liturgical worship that followed printed word-for-word exchanges between the pastor and the people? Was it a freer pattern with no liturgy? Was it along the lines of a folk service?

Follow your telling of your experience with this short mini-drama using three of the group as readers.

THE STATE OF THE CHURCH

SETTING: Peter, James, and John have just returned to heaven after a brief scouting trip to Earth to examine the church as it is today. They are informally discussing their experiences before making their formal reports.

PETER: Hey, fellas, how did your inspections go?

JOHN: I don't mind saying that I certainly had my eyes opened! Why, I could hardly believe that I was looking at the same church that we started.

PETER: I know what you mean. I went into First

Lutheran and discovered that a man by the name of Martin Luther was trying to introduce some reforms into the Catholic church, and when it all ended, he had started a new church instead of reforming the one to which he belonged.

JAMES: I found that out, too. But it didn't stop there! Some other men came along: men named Calvin, Wesley, and Williams, and the church moved in many different directions. I just don't see how anyone can keep them all straight. Why, you never saw such a listing of names! Roman Catholic, Eastern Orthodox, Presbyterian, Lutheran, Baptist, Methodist, Pentecostal, Mennonite, and the United Church of Christ, to name only a few.

JOHN: I couldn't keep straight which one I was in without looking at the name at the top of my bulletin. It was confusing, because I didn't know if I should kneel or stand or just sit there.

PETER: I got in on a couple of baptismal services. They were surely different from the ones we all did. In one these people brought their baby, and the minister sprinkled some water on her head. The other was the baptism of an adult, and he went down into a tank of water with the minister who immersed him completely under the water.

JOHN: I got to see a couple of those, too. It seems that they feel it is all in how you interpret the Scripture. Some feel that baptism is what brings you into God's grace.

JAMES: Not to change the subject, but did either of you see a Communion service? One time I had to go to the front of the church and kneel, while at another I stayed in the pew and was served by the person next to me.

JOHN: I was at one service and went forward and received only the bread. The minister was the only one who got any wine.

PETER: I was at one where they washed my feet as I came into the church before having Communion. I wonder how they tell when to have Communion. It seemed to me that some churches were having it every week, and others were having it only once a quarter.

JAMES: Seems like I'm the one always changing the subject, but I noticed that in some churches all the people joined together in singing some hymns while in some others the only persons who sang were a few people off by themselves with the minister.

JOHN: I got into one church where the people enjoyed their singing so much they must have been heard clear up here.

PETER: The one church I remember was one where they didn't have any musical instruments to accom-

pany the people as they sang. But that didn't seem to bother them, because they really sang. Say, did either of you get into one of those churches where they don't have any ministers; but you all sat down together in meditation and then if anyone had anything to say, he would say it; or if anyone wanted to pray, he just started praying? That was a moving experience!

JAMES: Needless to say, I think we all discovered that the church has certainly undergone some changes from the times when we were leading it. It has moved in so many directions through reforms or by trying something new and different. I think in our final report we need to note that there are certainly a lot of churches and each is different; and the ministry is approached a little differently, but they are all involved in bringing Jesus Christ and his message of God's love into the world.

PETER: I think you are right, James. No matter what form of worship, what practice of Communion and baptism, or what kind of governing body, each was ministering as it saw the need of the people around the church.

JOHN: It really made me feel good that, even though they were different in approach, they were all reaching for the same goal. People are surely different, and they can all find a style of church and ministry that is going to appeal to them so they can serve Jesus as each of us has done.

Following the end of the mini-drama, you may wish to ask the group what differences were mentioned. Also ask if there were any differences which they have noticed that were not mentioned.

Approach B

Begin by sharing one of your experiences in worshiping in a church of another denomination. Point out the differences that you noticed, and explain why they might exist. Allow time for each of the group to share a similar experience in another church. In each case try to get behind the differences to see why they might exist. To do this, you will need to have some general knowledge of the other denominations. You may also wish to bring out some of the aspects of how the different denominations came about through the Reformation and later reforms and splits. Check with your pastor for resource information on this or consult *A Short History of Christianity* by Martin E. Marty.[1] Also in this approach you might want to investigate

[1] Martin E. Marty, *A Short History of Christianity* (Cleveland: Meridian Books, imprint of World Publishing Company, 1959).

some of the forms of church government, that is, Catholic with their bishops and pope as compared to the congregational form of the Baptists and the United Church of Christ. Conclude by noting that each church is involved in a ministry to serve Jesus Christ according to its interpretation of Scripture and traditions.

DEALING WITH DIVERSITY

Look at these passages from Paul. Each is dealing in a way with the church and can probably be applied to the larger realm of all the churches of Jesus Christ and their relations to one another. There are many other passages which you may use here; so select from these or ones of your own choice.

1 Corinthians 12:12-31. In this passage the author is trying to point out the interdependence of all the parts of the body for the body to function as it properly should. In relation to the many denominations, one might look at this from the aspect that each denomination has a vital function with its people, but without the functions of the other denominations it cannot fully be the body of Christ. We are different, and yet we must work together if we are to complete the ministry of Christ.

Ephesians 4:1-16. This passage is similar to the first one but notes the different gifts that each has received. We as denominations have different gifts that we can use in our ministry, but we serve the same Christ, having received the same Spirit, and belong to the one body. Each gift is necessary, and one without the other is incomplete.

Ephesians 2:11-22. This passage tells us what Christ has done for us and *all* humankind. There is no distinction in the eyes of Christ, but all are the same. We are all building upon the same foundation as we minister in our world today.

Conclude this section with a couple of examples of denominations working together. Draw out of the discussion of the Bible passages the conclusion that we must work together to become fully the body of Christ.

CONCLUSION

There are many denominations within the church of Jesus Christ. Each denomination is involved in telling the gospel of Jesus Christ and seeking to carry out his ministry within our world. The denominations are not all alike because people are not all alike. The Scriptures allow for differences in styles of ministry and different approaches to the telling of the gospel. Yet there is a common goal that each is seeking to attain, and that is the sharing of the love of God for every person. Because our styles of ministry, our forms of worship, and our church governments vary, the style and form of any one church will appeal to some people whereas the style and form of another church appeals to other persons. Therefore we have many denominations, each in its own way seeking to bring God's love revealed through Jesus Christ to our world.

FURTHER SESSION IDEAS

1. Ask a panel of four or five different pastors to come and share some of their history and beliefs and how they worship. Allow for the young persons to ask their questions. Perhaps they may wish to write their questions down before the session begins.

2. Take several sessions to visit other churches/worship services. Make arrangements with the pastor to meet after the service to answer questions the youth may have.

3. Spend some sessions looking into church history to see how the denominations were formed through splits, reforms, and other means. You, as the leader, will have to do almost all of the research and then pass it on to the group. (See resource suggestion under Approach B.)

Lon Schneider is pastor of the First Baptist Church, New Hampton, Iowa.

PRACTICING RELIGIOUS DISCIPLINE

Prayer, Bible study, and worship that are relevant

by DAVID J. BAN

WHY?

Today's youth often have difficulty relating to traditional religious disciplines in modern settings. A frequent complaint of youth group leaders is that they can't seem to "get the kids interested" in some of the things that they feel are important to their faith: prayer, Bible study, and worship. What is often missing is the understanding that these experiences can happen in ways which are less traditional and more relevant to where youth are.

This is a plan for a retreat with junior highs that offers a flexible format for active exploration of new ways of approaching one's religion. It is meant to be as much of an adventure as it is a "retreat" and should be approached as an experience in which the youth and the leaders participate equally as learners.

THE SETTING

An elaborate setting isn't important in making a retreat worthwhile. The important thing is that your group has a place where it can be together, interact, and play together for two or three days. Some things to consider are: Where do we sleep? How will we eat? Is there someplace where we can meet together as a group? There needs to be a place big enough to hold the whole group, yet small enough for everyone to be comfortable. It's more fun to be someplace with room for adventure—outdoors, near a lake, in a city, at the beach. With a little imagination, even the basement of the church can be an arena for adventure. The idea of a retreat is partly to "get away from it all," but even more importantly, to have an opportunity for the group to share some time learning and thinking about things in new and different ways.

WHAT TO BRING

Where your group decides to go will determine what you need to bring. Of course, you should plan to make use of the things provided naturally at your location. For instance, if you are at the beach, you could make sand candles or driftwood mobiles. In a wooded setting, plant or leaf pressings might be fun. The point of arts and crafts is to get involved with the setting. Craft activities should allow for group involvement and individual expression.

Some real necessities are a record player, some favorite records, songbooks, guitars, lots of large-size newsprint, Magic Markers, and crayons. You will also want to make some beforehand provisions for food. Food planning can have adventuresome possibilities: anything from a taffy pull to pizza-making to a big spaghetti feast.

Don't forget, of course, the standard Frisbees, basketballs, footballs, Twister games, and softball gloves!

SCHEDULE

The schedule should be flexible. A good portion of time can be profitably spent just having fun. In most activities it is really important that everyone feels involved. When this is an understood goal, all sorts of things can become festive and frivolous and worthwhile.

There should be some times specifically set aside for "input sessions," which can range from Bible study to nature walks to sing-alongs to a movie or speaker. Setting mealtimes and sharing some duties (cooking, setting tables, cleanup, etc.) are also important.

SETTING GUIDELINES

Rules are often burdensome and seem to be made to

be broken. Bedtimes are seldom if ever kept. It really doesn't make sense to get out a long list of rules and regulations. Instead a house "contract," an understanding of mutual responsibility, may find a more eager acceptance. Here are examples of three flexible guidelines for living in a community:

1. Don't do anything to hurt yourself or anyone else—as a community we must care for each other.

2. Clean up after yourself—as a community, we share this space.

3. No folding, spindling or mutilating—as a community we have a commitment to care for each other's feelings, and to be serious and honest in our dealings with the group.

SOME PROGRAM INPUTS

Here are some activities which may stimulate thinking and involvement. They are on a wavelength with junior highs and are meant to be experiment-adventures in some of the traditional disciplines of the church.

An Opening

In this exercise, the group has as its purpose making the meeting room its own space. Everybody, including the leader-facilitators, gets a piece of large newsprint and chooses a colored Magic Marker (or several for that matter). The leader gives instructions that go something like this: "This room is going to be our 'space' for this retreat. It is the 'home base' for all of our explorations and adventures. To make it seem like our space, we're going to make these special signs. Here's the task: On your sheet of newsprint, make a 'picture' of yourself. This doesn't have to be a masterpiece—just make a picture of some of the things that are important to you right now."

After this is done, each person can share his or her drawing/creation, with the group. With a piece of masking tape, place the picture wherever each person thinks it belongs in that room. In its own way, this is a serious exercise. Persons are being called on to share something of themselves with the group; and though that sharing may be simple, it is important.

When this exercise is finished, group members can share some of their hopes for the retreat and some of the plans and schedules. This can be an opportunity for making clear the guidelines and responsibilities of each person.

Bible Study

Bible study doesn't have to be stuffy and boring. It doesn't have to be done sitting down, either. Here is a suggested role play that can put some life into two old and well-known Bible stories:

1. **Read Matthew 19:16-23,** the story of the rich man wanting to know how he was to gain entrance into the kingdom of heaven.

Here is a suggestion for a different setting, but with the same characters and the same situation. A description of the roles is given, but the dialogue is up to the role-players, who are members of the group. They should feel free to act this out however they see fit.

The scene is under a tree in the middle of a park in a big city. There are three characters: Jesus, a disciple, and the rich young man. The rich kid drives up in a souped-up Chevy convertible with mag wheels and chrome on the sides. He is wearing platform shoes, a bright purple shirt, and Levi's. He gets out of the car and strolls up to Jesus and says something like: "Hey, man, I hear you come up with this new gig, like, that gets a dude a first-class ticket on a train of life; like kind of a guaranteed fix on the kingdom. Like, wow, man! Like I could really dig a piece of this action and like I was kind of wondering if you could spell out the rap for me. . . ." The players can then create Jesus' response to the rich young man.

2. **Read Luke 14:16-24,** the story of a man who gave a feast that nobody would come to. The characters for this role play will be the man throwing the party, his servant, and the people who are too busy to come. The dialogue can go something like this: The servant says, "Say, there, my boss is throwing a party and is having all sorts of good things and good people and is even barbequeing T-bones and making homemade ice cream. He'd like for you to come." The reply: "Like bug off, man, I've got a previous engagement, like this really bombed date. . . ."

Some questions to ask: Who is the rich man today? What does it mean when Jesus says, "Come, follow me"? Why did Jesus tell the parable of the banquet? When do we make excuses not to come? When do we cop out on Christ?

Prayer

Here is an opportunity for active participation in the act of praying. It is a symbolic acting out of a Bible verse, but in a much more serious tone than the role plays. While someone reads Matthew 25:34-40, the group members act out the giving of food, the clothing of the naked, the offering of shelter. This is meant to be a serious sharing of concerns and can take the form of a silent rhythmic dance. When the Scripture has been read, the group members can sit down again and, if they wish, can further share their concerns and cares for those in need, in the form of a litany. A concern is stated, and the group responds with "As you did this to the least of these . . . you did it to me."

A Creative Worship Service

For this worship service there is a time of preparation during which the participants are given a chance to create their contribution to the service. As members of the church, we share in an enterprise of exploration, commitment, and adventure. The worship service is a way of celebrating the adventure, reaffirming the commitment, and renewing the exploration.

The group meets as a whole and is broken into subgroups of three. Each group is assigned a task. Here are some possible tasks:

1. Create a song about belonging to this particular group.

2. With newsprint and Magic Markers (or felt and glue if you have time), make a big banner that tells about this retreat and what we have learned.

3. Create a litany sharing our concerns for the world.

4. Decorate the room for a celebration (balloons, flowers, etc.).

5. Using whatever you can find, make a sculpture that is symbolic of the church.

6. Dance out a prayer of thanksgiving (to music if you want). There can be about forty-five minutes for these tasks, after which all in the group come together and share their contributions. At the end of this sharing, perhaps some further statement about what has been learned, what has happened, and what yet needs to be done could be shared.

David J. Ban is a student at Kalamazoo College, an American Baptist-related institution.

PROJECT

COMMITMENT THROUGH CHURCH INVOLVEMENT

Acting on the mission in the church

by DAVID A. BROWN

POINT OF VIEW

Projects may start with discussion, but they have a flavor in their design which invites participants to act on what they say they believe, and to act on what they say they value. This kind of action brings wholeness to education because learning is moved to the gut level of emotions. You can discuss a hiking trip and look at maps and even learn the names of valleys and mountains, but you do not really know that lake or mountain until you actually go there and see and feel it; then you really understand that map. Our faith is our map, taking actions on our faith is the experience which brings wholeness to our Christian education.

Projects need to invite participants to take action during the week in addition to your regular weekly youth meeting. This extra involvement or the lack of it is a key measuring device of the youth's enthusiasm for the project at hand. Also, this enables maximum involvement and productivity within a relatively short time. Let an event drag on much longer than a month with junior highs, and interest is replaced by endurance.

PURPOSE

To help junior highs explore and express their commitment through involvement in their church's mission.

PROCEDURE

Step 1

Take some "pictures" of your church's mission.

One picture of the church's mission can be developed by having the youth brainstorm what they think the mission or purpose or job of the church is. At the end of the brainstorming session, ask them to choose which things are most important. List items in the

> **WHY?**
>
> The youth need to understand what the mission of the church is before they can make an intelligent commitment to it. The very act of clarifying what the mission of the church is will be helpful, should the youth choose to accept this assignment. (If they do not, the church may self-destruct in a matter of years.)

order of importance; then ask what kinds of grades they would give the church for actual performance on the various items listed. Suggest that the youth ask their parents what they think the mission, purpose, or job of the church is, and bring back the various answers. The parents could also be asked to grade the church's performance.

A second picture of your church's mission would be through what your pastor does. Have group participants think through all their questions about what a minister does on behalf of the church, and bring him or her into a session with the group where they can ask their questions. If you have a multiple staff, such as a minister of Christian education, or a minister of music, these persons could also provide pictures of the church's mission.

These last two pictures of the church's mission could be formally "framed" with a ceremony dedicating the "Youth Officers for the Month."

A third picture of your church's mission could be developed through seeing what some of your church officers and leaders do. Ask the youth what they think the responsibilities of these leaders and their boards or committees are. Decide on how many of these leaders will be actually studied, and let youth choose the leader they will study. Let them draw straws, or you draft them, whichever is appropriate for your group. Often it will be best to allow youth to form teams of two or

20

three students to give them courage for a face-to-face encounter with an adult who is neither a teacher nor a relative. Assign the youth to interview their leaders about their responsibilities and then actually to sit through a meeting with the leader's board or committee. If the counselors contact these leaders beforehand and explain the purpose of these projects, it will make it easier for the junior highs to call and set up the interview and meeting.

The fourth picture of your church's mission can be developed by studying your church's budget. You could do this to see the areas of work in which your church is involved. Also, those in your group who are mathematically inclined could figure up the percentage of the budget which goes to missions, to church programs, to the building, etc.

Step 2

Report back.

> ### WHY?
>
> Here is where learnings of one student can spark or clarify learnings for another student. It also is a key time for evaluating, if the youth have come to the realization that the church's mission is not carried out just by the pastor, but by parents and by themselves; for they are not only the church's youth group. The church, rather the church's mission, is theirs, because they are the church.

Have the students report back the understandings gained of what the mission of the church really is and how it is carried out. Depending on the size of your youth group, this is usually best done in small groups of five or six followed by the small groups reporting their observations to the entire group. Especially seek to understand if and in what ways their understanding of the church and its mission has changed.

Step 3

Take action. Find out what the junior highs liked and admired about their church's mission. Send thank-you and congratulation notes to the people, boards, and committees which they admired. Brainstorm to find ways to help. Even if no ways of helping are found, the act of saying thanks and well-done is a ministry in itself and one not at all overdone in the church.

Also, find out what the junior highs did not like or what they thought needed improvement. If the youth divided into teams, there might be several smaller projects carried out by two to eight people, but try to have at least one project that would be worked on by the total group. For example, raise funds in support of one of your church's mission projects as listed in the church budget; or raise funds for an item not in the budget which your study concluded should be, such as camperships which would pay up to half the cost of camp for some youth. This type of fund-raising project could result in a new item being included in next year's budget, reflecting your youth's involvement in expanding your church's mission.

IF YOU HAVE MORE TIME
(Or how to expand the suggestions above.)

Step 1

A much more detailed "close-up" of the church's mission could be taken by electing a couple of representatives to go with the pastor on a series of hospital calls, calling on the bereaved as well as attending a funeral service, and sitting in on a premarital counseling session (with the permission of the couple involved) as well as the actual wedding. The sit-in observations would provide the best kind of experiential learning of the mission of the church. You might elect different teams to go on the hospital calls and the call on a bereaved person. As well as letting more students in on these kinds of experiences, people may be at different readiness levels. Some may be ready for hospital calls, but not ready for the intimate closeness to death which a call on the bereaved would mean.

When considering the work of boards and committees, it would be good for youth to go with some boards and committees who do things outside the monthly meetings. For example, the diaconate or some group has responsibility for visiting shut-in members. Have a couple of youth go with the adults on such a visit. Perhaps the trustees have a work-project coming up, or perhaps the Christian education board is planning an event with which youth could help, such as an art day for children.

Although some churches have youth as regular members of various boards, often these youth do not communicate with other youth about what goes on; so do not be afraid to assign a youth officer to a board that has a youth as a regular member.

Step 2

Schedule a "Parents' Night In," or a Parent/Counselor Session. Call it what you will, but use the occasion for the students to report and discuss with parents their findings. You could think through **Step 3** with the parents.

Rev. David A. Brown is Minister of Christian Education of the First Baptist Church, Lafayette, Indiana, with responsibilities for administering all phases of the educational ministry.

DISCOVERING OTHER DENOMINATIONS

Group research into the why's and what's of denominations

by DAVID A. BROWN

PURPOSE

To help junior highs understand differences among denominations.

> ### WHY?
>
> We can come to understand ourselves better as we try to understand others. By meeting face to face with youth from other denominations, we can come to understand our distinctives within the perspective of our common purpose.

PROCEDURE

Step 1: Where Did We and They Come From?

Have your youth and the youth from one or two other denominations do a brief bit of research into the history of their own denomination and put this into the form of a ten to fifteen minute play, to be presented on a mutually agreeable date.

> ### WHY?
>
> This would get into the content, but in such a way that there could be creative roles for the non-verbal kids as well as the verbal ones.

Those who have a way with words can take notes from history books[1] and/or an interview with your pastor and can work on scripts. Others can make costumes, sets, and lighting. These can be as elaborate as you have personnel and interest, but often a very

[1]See Martin E. Marty, *A Short History of Christianity* (Cleveland: Meridian Books, imprint of World Publishing Company, 1959).

simple set will be the best. Have an intermission (complete with pop and popcorn) after each play with some time for informal discussion. Conclude the evening with a more formal discussion of the plays in small groups. Try to keep the small groups mixed with two or three youth from each denomination.

Two possible discussion questions are: (1) What were some of the goals of the original founders? (2) In what ways, if any, has the denomination changed since its beginning?

Step 2: Worship Styles

Have five or six youth from one of the denominations you are studying visit your church in worship. Try to arrange this on a Sunday with Communion or baptism, as these tend to be key areas of differences. Have them meet with your young people afterwards in a special lunch over hamburgers from the nearest quick service restaurant or invite them to that evening's youth meeting. Have them ask your youth why they do things the way they do, from the way people are greeted and called to worship, to the way the hymns are introduced and the way people are dismissed. Have the visitors share their impressions and feelings. What helped them worship God? What interfered or caused confusion?

This series could be climaxed with a session with the pastor to work on areas of confusion that remain.

Follow this up with a visit of your youth to the church of your guests, or to yet another denomination. Again, meet afterwards, this time in their church to discuss similar questions on why things were done the way they were and what helped or hindered their worship of God.

IF YOU HAVE MORE TIME

1. After completing your tour of different styles of worship, plan and carry out your own worship service,

either leading the entire congregation in worship or a separate service for the youth and parents.

2. In a retreat setting, invite a pastor or lay person from another denomination to lead your youth in worship. A Saturday night formal worship with written liturgical prayers and congregational responses could be very moving if your youth are not used to this. Perhaps you would rather conclude your weekend together with a Sunday morning Quaker or Plymouth Brethren style of worship in which individuals contribute to worship by testimonies, leading in prayer, or suggesting songs to be sung as they feel led to do by the Holy Spirit.

Rev. David A. Brown is Minister of Christian Education of the First Baptist Church, Lafayette, Indiana, with responsibilities for administering all phases of the educational ministry.

SECTION I
Program Resources
About Communication

BRIEF EXERCISES

RETREAT

SIMULATION GAME

EXPLORING COMMUNICATION SKILLS

Practice in listening, talking, understanding communication

by GARY L. REIF

This is a series of communication exercises allowing junior highs and their adult leaders to explore some technical ingredients of communication, and then to test their findings. They can be used as a series of weekly programs, or a combination of some of the exercises might be used in a retreat setting.

RESOURCES ANYONE?

Please look through this material and note particularly the book, *God Is for Real, Man*, by Carl F. Burke, and Clarence Jordan's record "The Rich Man and Lazarus," which you may need to order.

"Hello."
"Nice day, isn't it?"

"Hi! What happened at school today?"
"Ah—nothin'."

"Sue, how many times do I have to tell you to clean up your room?"
(Silence)

"John, that was a great touchdown run you made last night."
"Ah, thanks. But the hole between guard and tackle was something else! We should have a good team this year."

Today COMMUNICATION is a big word. What we say—what we hear—how we hear—what the rest of our body is saying while we're talking—the radio and TV commercial—news—pictures!

Wasn't the clarity of voice transmission in the first lunar space landing amazing? How did they do it? Through Telstar we watch track meets and hear news reports taking place on the other side of the earth. At the same time that we're communicating across thousands of miles, families are breaking up because husband and wife are unable to tell one another how they feel, or engage in a workable plan to resolve their differences. Youth become upset with their friends because they don't "catch" what is being said, or they hear "too well."

To be able to communicate is an art—it takes practice and desire to pull it off. How good a communicator are you? Would you like to help yourself and another person improve? That's what we're about in these exercises.

BUT BEFORE WE START DOING IT, let's find out what communication is.

EXERCISE I. LEARNING WHAT WE MEAN BY COMMUNICATION

There's an important distinction between the mere act of transmitting information, conversation, or simple interchange of thoughts and opinions, and an interaction between persons who understand each other, who are on the same "wavelength."

Communication takes place when one person tells something to another, and what the second person hears is what the first person intended to say.

Better stop and discuss this sentence! What does it say?

What does it communicate to you?

Check out this definition by turning to one person near you and sharing one thought expressed in a sentence or two. (Such as: "What unusual thing happened at school this week?") After you speak, have your friend tell you what he/she heard and vice versa.

Did you find yourself listening more carefully than usual? Did you find yourself choosing the *best* words to express what you wanted to say? Did you use gestures to emphasize your ideas?

Don't become discouraged, for "perfect" communication seldom, if ever, occurs. Two persons will always understand a sentence differently. Rather, we should rejoice when a real meeting of meaning takes place, and when it does not, we should be challenged to extend ourselves in an honest effort to hear accurately. Perhaps you will need to analyze the situation in terms of the other person's life experience (cultural, educational, and social background), choose more wisely the words you use, and ponder more accurately the words she/he uses in return.

> COMMUNICATION doesn't happen all over the place; it's amazing that communication happens as often as it does!

The Communication Process

There are five steps necessary for communication to take place:

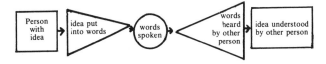

Let's say you want to tell someone else that the room is cold.

You begin with an idea: I feel cold.
You put this idea into words: It's sure cold in here!
You speak these words: It's sure cold in here!
The other person hears these words: It's sure cold in here!
The other person understands your idea: I guess that person feels cold.

Barriers to Communication

There are several things that get in the way of our communication. Here are some:

1. *Language:* Sometimes we use words that can have different meanings. Let's say that in the example above, instead of saying, "It sure is cold in here," you said, "I have goose bumps all over my arms." Some people might not understand what "goose bumps" are. Others might think that you had goose bumps, not because you were cold, but because you were excited. There are even more extreme examples of how language can get in the way of our communication. What about the use of teenage slang with an adult? If a youth says, "That guy looks cool," an adult who was a teenager during the fifties might think this teenager disapproved of the guy's looks. In the fifties, people talked about a "hot dish" rather than a "cool dude."

2. *Prejudice:* If you don't like the person with whom you are communicating, you may not hear what he/she is really saying. If someone you dislike says, "It sure is cold in here," you might think he/she is saying, "Why don't you turn up the heat?" You interpret his/her remark as a criticism, even though you were not openly criticized.

3. *Anxiety:* If you don't feel comfortable with another person, you may have difficulty speaking freely with him/her. Rather than mentioning that you are cold, you might just suffer.

4. *Defensiveness:* Most of us try to hide our own feelings at times. Instead of admitting that we are cold, we might say, "Why doesn't someone turn up the heat?"

5. *Different Purposes:* Some people only want to get their point of view across. They don't care what other people think. They choose not to hear someone who disagrees with them. To rely on our example, again, if we say, "It's cold in here" and someone else says, "I'm comfortable," we may not hear him/her.

Has this sounded HEAVY? Well, it really is! We're not going to be good communicators without knowing what's involved and then trying it. That's where we are now—let's try it.

EXERCISE II

1. Pair off in twos and discuss these questions:
   a. What's the most important thing going on in the world today?
   b. What's the most exciting thing in your life these days?
   c. What's your greatest concern?
   d. What's your strongest hope?

2. Now have the person you communicated with share with the group or with six or eight others the answers you gave to one or more of these questions. Then you report the information received from your friend. (DON'T let this part of the exercise be known beforehand!)

3. In groups of four, discuss what happened. Were you satisfied with the way your friend reported to the group on your behalf? What errors or omissions were made in the receiver's report? How do you feel about this? What went wrong in the communication process? What was good about it? How could it be better?

4. With this experience, you might want to try a second round of questions, choosing those you did not

use in the first round or making up some new ones ahead of time.

EXERCISE III

Some of the most effective communication occurs in radio and TV commercials. What are commercials saying to us, trying to make us believe? How are they doing it?

1. Have the group view a series of commercials between two TV shows. This shouldn't take more than ten minutes if you tune in on the hour or half-hour. *OR* have several youth explain in detail one of their favorite commercials which the group should easily recognize.

2. In groups of three of four discuss:
   a. What are the commercials assuming about me—the audience?
   b. What do they want me to believe or know?
   c. What are they telling me, and not telling?
   d. How are they doing it (catchy music, funny cartoon characters, lovely scenery, etc.)?

3. Discuss as an entire group: what commercial was best—why?

4. (This is a little different kind of question, but you might like to get into it.) Are commercials fair? Should there be more control over what can be advertised and how it can be advertised? Do you agree with the ruling on banning cigarette advertising?

5. Have small groups think of ways to say something to someone via a commerical. Describe it and/or act it out. Evaluate what happened. What communicated best to you? Why?

EXERCISE IV

One of the most lengthy and regular attempts at communication in the church is the pastor's sermon. What do you get from it? How well do you listen? How effective a communicator is your pastor? How might you be able to assist your pastor in the communication process? Let's find out.

In consultation with your pastor, plan a sermon talk-back OR as a group work on this project and share your findings with your pastor.

Plan One

1. Meet with your pastor in his or her study, or invite him or her to your group. Share with your pastor your objective in learning to become better communicators.

2. Ask your pastor to share how he or she goes about the task of preaching. Let the pastor know about this question when the invitation to talk to your group is given. You will learn something about your pastor as a person as well as certain techniques in developing a sermon. This knowledge should aid communication later on.

3. Discuss your response to the following questions which you have written down or thought about from a recent sermon (the more recent the better).
   a. What did the pastor say to you? (The question is not: What did the pastor say?)
   b. What difference, if any, do you think the message you heard will make to you in your relationships?
   c. In what ways did the pastor's method, language, illustrations, and delivery help or hinder your hearing of the message?
   d. What relation did you see between the worship and the preaching?
   e. Did you help the pastor preach the sermon? Explain.

4. Ask your pastor for an answer to question "*a*," and what he or she hoped for in terms of "*b*" and "*d*" above.

5. What forms of worship and preaching contribute more than others to good communication? Why or why not? How concerned are we in the church about communication?

6. Have two or three persons, including the pastor, evaluate what has been learned about communication through this exercise. The whole church should benefit—including you and your pastor!

Plan Two

If the pastor cannot be involved in your discussion, have the group write down and/or discuss responses to the five questions above. Note how different persons hear different things. Why is this true? How can we become better participants in the communication process at church?

EXERCISE V

An exciting way to work at better communication is to translate a Bible passage or story into your own language. The familiarity of the language has caused some contemporary translations of the Bible, such as *Good News for Modern Man, The Living Bible,* and *The Cotton Patch Version of Paul's Epistles* by Clarence Jordan, to be so popular.

Plan One

Carl F. Burke, chaplain of Erie County Jail in Buffalo, New York, wrote a book, *God Is for Real, Man.*[1] It is a translation by kids from the city streets of well-known Bible passages and stories, written while they were in jail. Get a copy of this book, read a story from it, and then read the corresponding story in the regular translation of the Bible you use. What are the differences? How does the translation or paraphrase in Burke's book enable you to understand the Bible story better, or doesn't it?

Plan Two

Divide up into groups of three or four, and have each group select a Bible passage to put in contemporary words. Share the work of each group with the larger group. What happened? What's the value of paraphrasing? How could this technique be used more often in the church?

Plan Three

Secure a copy of one of Clarence Jordan's records in which he tells one of the parables of Jesus using contemporary language in a present-day rural, southern setting. "The Rich Man and Lazarus" or "The Great Banquet" are ideal.[2] Again compare this with a reading of the same story from the Bible. How is communication strengthened or weakened? Divide into groups of four to six and try putting a parable in the setting of your city, school, and life. Share your work with the group.

[1]Carl F. Burke, *God Is for Real, Man* (New York: Association Press, 1966).
[2]Both produced by Koinonia Records, 617 Custer Street, Evanston, IL 60602.

Plan Four

Discuss what a parable is and how Jesus used the parable so effectively in his ministry. (Have an outside leader present this, or have a special research report by a youth. Look up "parable" in a Bible dictionary.) This was perhaps Jesus' best means of communication!

Have small groups of five to seven select an issue or concern in life today, and develop a parable about it. Perhaps the contemporary parable will fit in one of the following categories which encompass most of the New Testament parables: (*a*) A new thing God has done in the world through Jesus, (*b*) the character of the disciple, (*c*) God's love and forgiveness, (*d*) readiness for the end time. Share your work by having someone tell or read the story while others act it out.

EXERCISE VI

Using what you have learned about communication, participate in a small group discussion about the following questions. Speak clearly, and to the point. Use language you feel others in your group can understand. Listen closely while others speak. Ask questions if the meaning is not clear. Check out with one another "what you heard me say" if you're in doubt whether you're getting your meaning across or not.

1. What age would you like to be for the rest of your life?
2. If you lost everything you own, what would you do?
3. If you had just twenty-four hours to live, how would you spend them?
4. If you were in a serious jam, to whom would you go for help?

Rev. Gary L. Reif is minister of the Federated Church, West Lafayette, Indiana.

IMPROVING INTERGENERATIONAL COMMUNICATION

Junior highs and adults can understand each other

by VINCENT H. COLETTA, JR.

Junior high youth are related to adults in everyday life—parents, teachers, store clerks, athletic coaches, police, librarians, church workers with youth, and ministers. But many are not at ease in these relationships. It seems to be easier for many youth and adults to relate to those approximately their own age. People are conditioned for this in several ways, one of which is the graded school system for children and youth which continues on through university and beyond into adult vocations. In graded classes and in most adult jobs persons relate mostly to others their own age. But above and below one's own age level there is much to be learned from one another. This retreat plan suggests ways to improve these intergenerational relationships.

PROPOSAL: AN INTERGENERATIONAL RETREAT IN FOUR PHASES

1. **Exploration Phase.** A representative group of junior high youth, workers with youth, and parents (or other adults who will be at the retreat) develop a statement of purpose, plan of procedure, and tentative schedule.

2. **Discovery Phase.** A procedure is used to discover and collect data on how youth and adults presently feel about their own human situations and how they feel toward those above or below their age.

3. **Realization Phase.** Opportunity is provided to

WHY?

Retreats may have a modest effect because while the expectancy of discovery and exploration is usually fulfilled as part of the retreat weekend, the realization of actual growth experiences may not be included. This retreat has as the focal point the realization, preceded by the exploration and discovery and followed by actualizing new potentials of intergenerational relations in continuing activities.

---

experience what was discovered in data collection by being with one another at an overnight or weekend retreat where there is sufficient time to play, talk, reflect, eat, and live with one another.

4. **Actualization Phase.** Following the retreat, there are opportunities to plan continuing intergenerational experiences where we actually have extended peer experiences beyond the usual peer closeness.

RESOURCES NEEDED

1. Two portable tape recorders with several tapes. Check equipment to assure adequate audibility.

2. Large newsprint and felt-tip pens.

3. Location for the retreat. An outdoor church or community retreat center. A residence adequate for group meals, overnight lodging (floor space and sleeping bags), and an area for light recreation. An outdoor park or beach setting (not too crowded) where the group may spend day and overnight camping.

4. A representative group of junior high youth, workers with youth, and other adults who will attend retreat sharing development and responsibilities, such as:

   a. Dating the four phases
   b. Registrar and enrollment leaders
   c. Resource and equipment leaders
   d. Schedule coordinator
   e. Recorders for essential notes to be taken at each phase
   f. Development of a statement of purpose which will be explored, discovered, realized, and actualized. (Each of these phases will be explained with a detailed model.)

PHASE I: EXPLORATION

A representative group of junior high youth, workers with youth, and parents (or other adults who will be at retreat) with youth develop a STATEMENT OF PURPOSE about selves and others to be explored, discovered, realized, and actualized.

AN EXAMPLE STATEMENT OF PURPOSE:

We will try to discover how we presently relate to one another across generations and improve our communication with one another.

In this experience both youth and adults will attempt to:

describe their own world (their life situation as they feel and see it);
describe the world of one another (as youth and adults view and feel one another's world; as each feels the other views his/her world).

We plan to help persons at either age level to have: desirable, promising, and fulfilling experiences with one another—in fellowship, understanding, communication, playfulness, friendship, work, worship, and continuing relationship.

PHASE II: DISCOVERY

Church school time is most advantageous for discovery. Most churches have a junior high class and an adult class. A four-week block of time may be set aside prior to the retreat to discover present feelings related to the statement of purpose given above.

A procedure for data collection and orientation will be suggested that adequately records the present levels of attitudes, perspectives, feelings, fellowship, communication, and relations in the respective group at your church.

First Sunday

Adults and youth meet at their usual separate class sessions. Each group is asked to tape the most immediate thoughts and responses that come to their minds in questions such as:

ADULT CLASS

What do I feel my world is like—

as an adult?
as a mother?
as a father?
as a minister?
as a teacher?

as a scout or athletic leader?
as a truck driver, merchant, banker, manager, physician, or other adult vocation?

What are my hopes, dreams, worries, hurts, concerns, joys, disappointments, and fulfillments?

JUNIOR HIGH CLASS

What do I feel my world is like—

as a junior high youth?
as a public school student?
as a son or daughter?
as a brother or sister?
as a friend or alone?

What are my hopes, dreams, worries, hurts, concerns, joys, disappointments, and fulfillments?

Second Sunday

In separate sessions, not having heard each other's first taping, record answers to the following:

ADULT CLASS: As an adult, my image of the junior high world and their human situation is....
JUNIOR HIGH CLASS: As a junior high youth, my image of the adult world and their human situation is....

Third Sunday

In separate sessions, the adult tapes are listened to by the youth and the youth tapes are listened to by the adults.

There is an understanding that responses will not be given across age levels at church or at home until the day of the retreat. In fact, in this third session there is no time for responses within the separate groups because the tapes listened to represent two previous sessions to be heard in one session. For more meaningful listening there could be an early breakfast at church, followed by earlier-than-usual class sessions.

Fourth Sunday

In separate sessions, each group appoints a recorder who lists on newsprint the responses of the adults to the youth tape and responses of youth to the adult tape.
● There should be a full listing of all attitudes, images, and feelings as they come through to various persons in each group.

- All feelings, whether considered correct or incorrect, should be recorded.
- As true and authentic a response as possible should be recorded by each group as it heard and understood the other.
- This newsprint outline of each group is to be brought to the retreat with no communication to the other group as to contents until the initial sessions at the retreat.

PHASE III: REALIZATION

Though the place for the retreat may vary, it should be a place where experiencing one another is enhanced in playing, talking, eating, and living together.

The retreat will be an effective focal point for improving relationships only if there has been discovery and data collection as preparation for this phase of togetherness over the weekend.

Readiness to experience one another over a weekend of playing, talking, breaking bread with one another, and extended togetherness means a willingness to accept one another as revealed by the tape recordings, whether one agrees or disagrees with the attitudes expressed.

Adults in particular, and the youth as well, should give some thought to the wide expanse of feelings that will emerge in the weekend encounter. Neither adults nor youth should idealize their expectancies into some perfectionist impossibility. The expectations should be within the following possible movement of feelings:

1. Uncomfortable to comfortable
2. Timidness to openness
3. Unacceptance to acceptance
4. Ill at ease to ease
5. Misinformed to informed
6. Misunderstanding to understanding
7. Nondialogue to dialogue
8. Unempathic to empathic
9. Myth image to authentic image
10. Avoidance to initial fellowship
11. Age affinities to intergeneration affinities
12. Game-playing candidness to honest, but healing, candidness.

Friday Night Opening

If at all possible, some natural experiences of togetherness should take place (a meal together, refreshments, a get-acquainted game, light recreation, singing—a playful atmosphere that enhances ease of initial togetherness).

Session on Saturday

Listen to each other's composite newsprint report of each other's feelings:

1. Begin with adults on the questions youth dealt with on the first two Sundays of taping.

   a. Present the newsprint report.

   b. Have representative adults role-play two or three of the images they discovered on the tapes.

   c. Invite some natural responses from the youth.

2. Allow time for coffee and punch break. This should be long enough for mild exercise, walking, recreation, and games.

3. Have youth give their report in the same procedure as the adults—newsprint report, role playing, and some natural responses from the adults.

4. Arrange for lunch, followed by light recreational time.

5. Have small-group sessions in the afternoon if the size of the entire group is too large for common discussion. No group should have more than four youth and four adults, a total of eight. Each group should be a wise balance of youth and adults.

Adults are encouraged to be good listeners, helping to create an atmosphere of lively, candid expressiveness. In a therapeutic listening/responding atmosphere, natural feelings will be heard. The term "therapeutic listening" refers to that person who, when I am timid, makes me feel courageous; when I feel "not a part of the group," makes me feel at home; when I am ill at ease, makes me feel at ease.

Questions to be encouraged in the small-group sessions might include:

Do we have correct images of self and others?
Can we know correct images without being with one another?
Can we adequately relate to one another without really knowing each other's world of feelings?
Can adults learn from youth?
Can youth learn from adults?
Do we really know the hurts, joys, concerns, confidences, and other feelings of one another?
Are adults without such feelings because they are older?
Are youth without such feelings because their world has fewer problems?

6. Provide for evening dinner, followed by a warm fireside (indoor or outdoor) fellowship of singing in an atmosphere of love and acceptance that leads to a high proportion of open expressiveness as to what has happened to the group. Use these questions for evaluation:

a. What has happened to me and to us through this exploration, discovery, and realization at the retreat?

b. What, of a continuing nature, would I like to see actualized at our church, in my family, in our youth-adult group relations, and in my community?

(A person should be appointed to record these expressions, or they may be taped for use in the actualization design.)

PHASE IV—ACTUALIZATION

At home, after the retreat, a representative group reviews the expression of what happened at the retreat—along with some of the desired wishes for continuance of such patterns. There are two essential styles of continuance:

1. Each person may have realized improved relations in intergenerational experiences as the result of exploration, discovery, and realization that naturally becomes actualized in family life, church and community life.

2. Benefits should be sufficiently self-evident for a group to design continuing growth events of youth in relation to their minister, workers with youth, parents (and vice versa). Youth should be serving on church boards and committees, involved as participants in worship, intergenerational recreation events and extended family experiences.

Vincent H. Coletta, Jr., is minister of the First Baptist Church of Palos Verdes, California.

commUnIcation
—Everyone's a Winner!
commUNIcaTE

A game for teens to play with each other or with adults

by JACKIE JOHNSON

CommUnIcation is a game where everyone can be a winner. To be able to communicate what you think and feel is to win self-confidence. To be able to listen to others in order to understand what they think and feel is a personal gain. By sharing and listening we may be challenged to change our thinking and to *grow*.

WHY?

The aim of the game is to discover: Who Am I?—Who Do I Want to Be?—How Do Others See Me? While we are discovering these things about ourselves, we discover the same things about others who play the game. By playing the game, you will be able to clarify your stand on many questions, and perhaps you will be able to help others clarify their stand. There are no "right" or "wrong" answers in this game. No one has the whole truth; we each have a portion of it.

INTRODUCTION

* Anyone can play—especially good for adults and teens together.
* The best size of the playing group is four to eight persons. Divide larger groups into several small groups.
* Provide questions on colored cards for each group.
* The game can be played to a top score decided upon by the group, such as, "Tonight let's play to 30." Or it can be played to a predetermined time limit.
* The rules are guides only and can be changed by the group.
* The group players can add cards with their questions and situations.

TO GET READY TO PLAY

1. Questions should be typed (or duplicated if using more than one group), cut apart, and glued on colored cards according to their headings: PAST—red; NOW—yellow; FUTURE—green; HEAR THIS—blue.
2. Use a die for tossing each turn.
3. Each player needs a paper and pencil to record points at each turn.
4. You may want to write the scoring directions on newsprint so all can see.

RULES

Read the rules aloud before beginning play.
* The four piles of cards are face down in the center of the group.
* Each player throws the die. The one with the largest number begins.
* The first player throws the die. If it turns up:
1—Pick up a card from the top of the NOW pile and talk about it.
2—Pick up a card from the PAST pile. Two other players will ask one question each about the statement. Answer the questions and score two points. If there are no questions, score one.
3—Pick up a card from the FUTURE pile and talk about it (three points).
4—Pick up a card from the NOW pile, and two other players will ask the player one question each about that subject. Answer the questions and score four points. If no questions are asked, score two points.
5—Pick up a card from the HEAR THIS pile and answer it (five points). Anyone can ask you questions about your response. Each question answered is an additional point.
6—Pick up a card from the top of the HEAR THIS pile and answer it (six points).
* Each player marks his or her score on paper at the end of his or her turn. Play continues to the next person on the right.

* A player is not *required* to answer any questions. To pass, *do not* read the card aloud; place it at the bottom of the pile.

* Remember: There are no "right" or "wrong" answers.

Penalty. Any person who "pokes fun," "teases," or "laughs at" any person's answer deducts two points from his or her score.

Bonus. Any person, at the end of answering a question or statement, can call out: "Confront me." If others challenge this person with questions, another point is scored for each one answered.

HOW TO USE THE GAME

By itself the game can be a tool in communicating with one another—

* to clarify thoughts and verbalize feelings;
* to understand other points of view;
* to listen in order to understand another person better;
* to talk and question others without judgment;
* to involve adults and teens in the same feeling level;
* to get to know one another on a "deeper" level;
* to help develop a "group-ness" among those who participate.

The game can also be used as an exercise to follow the use of the program on dating (p. 47). It will help persons to experience sharing with others without using or manipulating them.

EVALUATE

At the end of the game take a few minutes for members of the group to share how they felt about the game. Ask each person to respond to the question "What did I learn about myself?" or tell "What did I learn about that I hadn't thought of before?"

IF YOU HAVE MORE TIME

CommUnIcation can be used as an exercise following the use of the program on the changing roles of men and women (p. 44). To vary the use, have the players ask questions dealing with the roles of men and women.

Example: A card off the PAST pile reads, "What I dislike the most." One answer could be, "Spoiled food smells." Questions from the others could be: "Who prepares the food most of the time at your house?" or "Do you do anything to help prepare food at home?" or "Do you ever spoil food?"

Example: A card off the HEAR THIS pile reads: "Do I like my name? Why?" One answer could be, "Yes, because I think it sounds pretty." Questions from the others could be: "If you were of the opposite sex, do you think you'd like your name?" or "Do you do anything differently because you have the name you have?" or "Who in your family, if anyone, favors you because of your name?"

Example: A card off the NOW pile reads: "My daydreams." Questions: "Could male or female do what your daydreams are about?" or "Do you ever dream of being the opposite sex? Why or why not?" "Who in your family or educational life gave you 'permission' to daydream?" or "Who, if anyone, told you daydreaming was bad?"

CARDS

These questions and statements are to be typed and pasted on colored cards according to the indicated headings. It is important that the questions come under the specific heading for continuity and clarity. One question per card.

PAST (red)

* What excites me most?
* What I dislike the most.
* The most fun I ever had.
* When did I last do something because of my faith?
* How do I feel when I am in the house alone?
* The feelings I have the hardest time expressing are . . .
* Tell about a time when my feelings were hurt.

* The last time I cried. Why?
* The foundation for my life has been . . .
* The person who has affected my life most is . . .
* One thing I missed in my childhood days was . . .
* A big let-down in my life was . . .
* My most embarrassing moment was . . .
* The happiest day of my life was . . .
* If I had pretended to be invisible at age ten, I would have gone to . . .
* A time I felt proud of myself.
* The neatest birthday present I ever got.
* The best thing about the past was . . .
* The best advice I ever received.
* What I disliked most about myself yesterday.
* My first impression of the person on my left.
* The best teacher I ever had and why.
* Describe myself as I was two years ago.
* Who changed my diapers the most?
* When I was six, who played with me more, Mom or Dad?
* Which grandparent have I seen the most in the past year?
* With whom do I relate better in my family, males or females?

HEAR THIS (blue)

* Do I like my name? Why?
* People receiving welfare checks should have to work. Why or why not?
* Public schools should teach religion. Why or why not?
* What makes a family happy?
* I have the power to give any gift in the world. What would I give to the person on my right?
* What activity do I do that involves all of me: my body, my soul, and my mind?
* If I could hang a poster in every home in the world, what would it be?
* Something I fear.
* Tell how I feel right now.
* Something I am "bugged" by.
* To me freedom is . . .
* Two things that make my life difficult.
* Define joy.
* Using one word, describe each player of this game.
* The "perfect" wife.
* The "perfect" husband.
* Something I feel sad about.
* Something I feel angry about.
* The talents I have.
* What I dislike most about me.
* An "ideal" child is . . .
* My favorite song.
* My favorite girlfriend.
* My favorite boyfriend.
* A frightening moment.
* The ideal life-style.
* The talent I wish I had.
* My favorite room in my home is . . . Why?

* People at sixty-five should be forced to retire. Why or why not?
* The trouble with our church is . . .
* Three good things about international missions.
* If I could be invisible, where would I go?
* Happiness is what color?
* I get "goose bumps" from . . .
* The best feeling I had today was . . .
* If I could be someone out of history, I would be . . .
* The worst thing parents can do to children.
* What I hope for when I'm sixty years old.
* I can make a long-distance phone call anywhere in the world. Whom will I call?
* I have the chance to win a five-foot trophy. What would I like it to be for?
* I have a good job. What are some reasons for leaving it?
* I am an animal in the zoo. What kind am I? What is my nickname?
* I was just driving down the road and I saw a hit-and-run driver. What will I do?
* I was driving down a residential street. A small child ran out in front of my car and is hit and hurt. What will I do?
* I wrote my autobiography. What title did I give it?
* What advice would I give my eighteen-year-old brother who is being married today?
* What my life will be like when I'm eighty years old.
* The material possession that will give me the most pleasure in twenty years.
* My best girl friend is getting married. What advice will I give her?
* I have the opportunity to live anywhere in the world. Where will it be? Why?
* If I could say anything I wanted to my pastor, it would be . . .
* If I could say anything I wanted to my father, it would be . . .

NOW (yellow)

* Death penalty for a murderer.
* Women have equal rights with men.
* Two good reasons for breaking the law.
* America—love it or leave it!
* Certain jobs for women only.
* Men who stay home all day while their wives work.
* Working women.
* Certain jobs for men only.
* Women who work and put their children in day-care centers.
* Husbands and wives who both work and share the cooking, cleaning, and child-caring jobs.
* The worst thing a person can do to another person.
* School.
* Describe a "good neighbor."
* My best friend (need not mention any names).
* How would I describe myself to someone who doesn't know me?
* Finish this: "I get tired of hearing . . ."
* Some kids using drugs.
* Say something about ghosts.
* A ten-year-old in my house should do what chores?
* Describe the "ideal" father.
* Describe the "ideal" mother.
* Describe a "good sport."
* Describe a "good loser."

* My daydreams.
* What I really believe in is . . .
* My parents and I.
* I'm prejudiced about . . .
* My sister/brother and I.
* What I value most in my life.
* Beauty is . . .
* Peace means . . .
* Three characteristics of my best friend are . . .
* A thing worth dying for.
* Obscenity.
* Mercy killing.
* What excites me about my faith.
* Using violence for changing society.
* Nude scenes in movies.
* Petting.
* Coed dormitories for college students.
* Birth-control pills.
* Birth control for unmarried teens.
* Violence in movies.
* Life's purpose is . . .
* Cigarette smoking.
* Use of "pot" and "grass."
* Getting drunk.
* TV advertising.
* Security is . . .
* Success is . . .
* The most sentimental possession I own.
* Three most important things in my life.

FUTURE (green)

* If I could be someone in the future, I would be . . .
* What kind of people are the luckiest people in the world?
* What do I think my friends say about me when I'm not around?
* What the world needs in 1999 is . . .
* What animal would I like to be and where would I live?
* What kind of job do I want twenty years from now?
* I am about to meet the president of the U.S.A. What one question will I ask?
* I was elected to work on the governing board at the church. What is the first change I will work toward?
* I would like to become famous by doing . . .
* What I think it is like to grow old.
* What ailment would I cure in the year 2000?
* What will I do in my spare time in 1999?
* I am told I have one week to live, and I am twenty-seven years old. How will I spend it?
* What will make my fiftieth birthday happy?
* I am a millionaire. Three things I will do with my money are . . .
* Missionaries should be sent home from foreign countries. Why or why not?
* I am a censor. What reasons can I give for censoring a nude movie?
* If I could say anything I wanted to my mother, it would be . . .

* My husband/wife just died and left me with three children, ages four, six, ten. What will I do now?
* I'm on a date, and my car ran out of gas on the expressway. What do I do now?
* My date asks me to "neck" and I don't want to. What do I say?
* My fifteen-year-old daughter is taking birth-control pills. As her parent, what do I say?
* I died at age seventy-five. What are my friends saying about me?
* A birthday present I'd like most to get.
* Magazines I will subscribe to in ten years.
* My date invited me to a "pot" party. I know it may get me in trouble with the law and my folks. What do I do?
* I can choose any life-style I want. It will be . . .
* I am invisible at a friend's party. What are they saying about me?

Jackie Johnson is a home-economics teacher in Merrill, Wisconsin, and a trainer in personal growth with youth, adults, and family-life groups.

SECTION I
Program Resources About Inner Struggles

GROUP STUDY

ART EXPERIENCES

PROJECT

RETREAT

SIMULATION GAMES

TO DOODLE, PERCHANCE TO FLUNK

How to deal with school pressures in junior high

by SHARON BALLENGER

WHY?

FOR ADULTS ONLY

Junior high is a shock to the psyches of many thirteen-year-olds. Moving from the sheltered elementary school environment where: (1) few demands were made; (2) most activities were carefully supervised—in many schools by one teacher per grade; and (3) rules were limited to such edicts as "only one potty break per day," the young person is often aghast at the difference when he or she enters the hallowed halls of junior high.

Suddenly in seventh grade, the student may be bussed to a much larger school, find eight teachers to please in one semester and a locker number to memorize. OR ELSE! A counselor begins giving choices (there had not been many until now) in terms of what courses to take next year, with the added reminder, "Be sure to come by next semester and we'll work out your high school schedule." The public library's declaration that one can now apply for an ADULT library card comes after the shocking realization that next year (he/she is counting the days), one can obtain a driving permit. Feelings of confusion, fear, and uncertainty create occasional yearnings in even the most stout of heart for a return trip to good old P.S. 101.

These changes combined with the changes in the body during adolescence naturally create some mental and emotional upheavals. A typical response emotionally to so much change so fast is to look for a way out. Escaping from assignments and responsibilities in school, the young person often adopts the following characteristics:

SKY HOOKING

On the surface the junior high appears in complete control. He gives the impression of being a lofty thinker with much imagination and maturity. Her head, however, is more often than not in the clouds, drifting, dreaming with no real goals or plans of action. No doubt, many sky hookers have creativity unlimited, but sooner or later those ideas have to be channeled, the energy harnessed, the hook secured in some solid turf.

SHOULDER SHRUGGING

The body language of this runaway drives many rational adults into the prenatal position. Suggestions, ideas, even questions are more often than not met with a shrug of the shoulder and a vacant stare. Whoever said "The opposite of love isn't hate, but indifference" had to have just come through an experience with a shoulder-shrugging eighth grader.

This program is designed for these runaways. No doubt, in the course of the evening, you, adult leader, will meet and recognize variations, combinations, and some new behaviors which you, with your wealth of talent may be able to tune in to, smile about, and begin to understand.

PURPOSE

The purpose of this program is to help junior highs look at the kinds of escapes they seek and to give them opportunities to explore options when a strong desire to run away again presents itself.

SETTING

The setting may be your normal meeting place. Or how about your house or the park (weather permitting)? A casual atmosphere is best. Floor sitting in recent years has threatened the chair manufacturer's livelihood but is recommended for facilitating an atmosphere of informality and warmth, and it encourages talking on a deeper level!

PROCEDURE

Step 1

As youth arrive, they are told to "get lost." This could be done by posting a sign on the door with the following message: DO NOT ENTER! ALL JUNIOR HIGH YOUTH ARE INSTRUCTED TO RUN AWAY SOMEWHERE IN THIS BUILDING. YOUR LEADERS WILL FIND YOU—BE QUIET AND DON'T GIGGLE! (Depending on the place, you may want to set bounds to limit the time required and/or for the sake of safety.)

Step 2

Meet back in the meeting area. Sit on the floor and discuss for a short time (5 minutes):

What were some of your feelings about running away? How many of you have ever really run away from home or school? How did that experience happen? What were your feelings? In school now, do you ever run away? If so, how? (Some responses will include "tuning out" the teacher, ignoring assignments, daydreaming, doodling, choosing "play" instead of work related to pressing deadlines.)

Step 3

Have group members show and tell, by making a collage, how they run away and what types of activities they run from.

Collage: What's That? Pictures cut from newspapers, magazines, plus a variety of other materials can be pasted on newsprint, cardboard, or construction paper to make a statement, express feelings, or tell a story—that's a collage.

Materials Needed. Scissors, paste, magazines, newspapers, bits of cloth, string, sand, sequins, newsprint, and cardboard or construction paper are needed.

Step 4

Come back to the group and have those who would like to do so share their collages.

Step 5

Have the group break up into pairs, go into huddles, and rap about other ways they *could* choose to behave when the tendency to run away again presents itself. These huddles could resemble brainstorms—firing suggestions at each other until each group member has one specific option he or she feels could be used the next time there seems to be a need to escape.

Step 6

Return to the group and on a large sheet of butcher paper hung on the wall (free, from your friendly neighborhood butcher) have the teams inscribe their new behavior. (This might be done by drawing pictures, writing short comments, or writing a limerick.) Example:

> There was a young lady from Glade,
> Who daydreamed a lot in eighth grade,
>   She gave up the habit,
> Learned lots about rabbits,
> And finished the year with all A's.

WHY?

Members of the group have individually admitted the ways in which they run away from important tasks. By getting together in groups of two and brainstorming, they have generated options (their own) for behaving differently. By writing them down, they have, in a sense, committed themselves to trying out the new behavior.

Step 7

Worship! Stand in a circle, join hands, and sing some joyful songs (for example "They Will Know We Are Christians by Our Love!", "Here We Are"). Have conversational prayer by different group members in a spontaneous way thanking God for each other, for gifts each has been given, and for the ability to discipline themselves to make the best possible use of those gifts.

IF YOU HAVE MORE TIME

Step 1

As youth arrive, have this message posted in the meeting area: (1) Write a letter to someone. (2) Scrub the floor in this room. (3) Read the book of Genesis.

Step 2

After they have had time to consider these assignments, have the group members share/respond to these questions:
1. Was I tempted to run away rather than to do one of the tasks?
2. Was one of the tasks more apt to suggest running away than the other two?
3. What feelings was I experiencing if thoughts of running away were in my mind?
4. Why did I want to run away?

Step 3

Invite a Bible resource person (pastor or minister of Christian education) to come in and give the youth opportunities to think about people in the Bible who ran away. (Good examples: Adam and Eve, Jonah, David, Lot's wife). Suggest that the consequences these people suffered were pretty painful.

Step 4

Divide the group into smaller groups of threes. Have each group take one of the biblical characters who ran away and rewrite the script, suggesting how the people in these situations could have behaved differently with more positive consequences.

EXAMPLE: The prodigal son ran away from commitments, responsibilities, and self-discipline. Instead, he could have—
1. Talked to his dad about his discouragement and unhappiness and suggested they try to work out their problems together.
2. Sought God's help through people by developing close relationships with trusting friends.
3. Worked at developing the gifts God had given him right at home (by "blooming where he was planted"!).
4. Taken a long vacation, checking out the world and gaining a new perspective in positive, meaningful ways.

Have each group assign roles when they have come up with a new "script." The group is not to write parts for the players, just describe the situation. The actors create dialogue as they play it. (A different twist might be to keep the situation a secret and have the rest of the group grope for clues during the action!)

Step 5

The leader says: "These situations happened a long time ago. What about you and what about now? An important thing to remember is that *you do have a choice in runaway situations*. You can sit in class and pay attention or you can [in your mind] escape to a surfing party. You can go to the library and study for the science exam or you can read the latest Harlequin romance."

Step 6

Play the song "Runaway" by Del Shannon (MCA, soundtrack from *American Graffiti.*). Have youth sit in a circle and listen quietly.

Step 7

Pray: "God help us to consider the choices we have carefully. Help us to choose LIFE by fulfilling our commitments and responsibilities." Amen!

Mrs. Sharon Ballenger is a high school counselor in Omaha, Nebraska.

AN AMERICAN MALE-FEMALE COLLAGE

The changing roles of women and men

by JACKIE JOHNSON

A LOOK AT SEX ROLES

Young teens in this changing society are faced with making decisions about their roles in life. Decisions about those roles may affect them and those with whom they associate for a long time into their future. This program is designed specifically to deal with sex roles, that is, the functions we assume because we are born male or female. Traditional examples of sex roles might be, "A woman's job is doing housework" or "Men don't cry."

Our sex roles are taught by family, tradition, society, culture, church, television, books, magazines, education, and practice. Often we are not aware that there are other behaviors than our own or that there are stereotyped ways of viewing sex roles. Becoming aware of the stereotypes is a step toward discovering the possibility of personal change and nature, personal choice.

PURPOSE: To identify sex roles, stereotyped or new, and to become aware of other choices we can make for the sex roles we assume.

WHY?

Often we are unaware of the advantages and disadvantages of sex-role expectations for the people of the opposite sex. To identify these sex-roles and to discover one's view of men and women may help us to become aware of other ways of viewing male and female roles. By becoming aware of sterotyped roles we can see other choices that we make for our own lives.

MATERIALS NEEDED

Many magazines, including those for family, men, women, and children; newspapers; paste or glue; large sheets of newsprint or paper (brown paper bags can be cut open and taped together); and tape to fasten the finished collages to the wall will be needed.

PROCEDURE

Step 1

Put the magazines, paste, and scissors out for the participants to use. Form two groups (same sex groups, if possible) and give each group a large sheet of paper.

Step 2

Introduce the exercise. Each group is to gather all the pictures or words or phrases that show sex roles most commonly found. The male group will make a collage of American women, and the female group will make a collage of American men. Each sheet of paper is to be divided in half with a mark or line. On the top left side write DO and on the top right side write ARE. (DO means jobs or hobbies or work, and ARE means characteristics or feelings they are known to express.)

Members in each group are to cut out pictures and words first, then as a group, they will decide if the pictures go on the *Do* or *Are* side before they paste them. Allow twenty-five to thirty minutes for the collage.

Step 3

When the collages are finished, each group can tape its collage up for all to see. Have the young women respond to the American women collage and the young men listen without defending or rebuttal. Then have the young men respond to the American men collage while the young women listen without defending or rebuttal.

WHY?

Sharing verbally without the listener having a chance to respond allows for more careful and less defensive listening.

Following the responses, the leader may want to provide guides to interpreting the collages and discovering the meaning of the activity. Suggested questions are:

Are all these jobs done only by men/women? Which jobs do you do? Do you fit the stereotypes? Where do we get the idea that these jobs are only for men/women? Where did we learn these stereotypes? Are these characteristics only male/female? Which ones are characteristics both sexes can have? Where did you learn that these characteristics or feelings were for men/women? What are some examples of changing sex roles that you know of from home? From the community? From school? From TV or ads? How are you changing your ideas about men and women?

Step 4

Have someone read these Scripture passages aloud: Romans 14:19; Ephesians 5:21; John 8:31-32. Have persons share what these passages say about our roles as persons, about our relationships with other persons—male or female.

In Closing

Help pull together some insights and learnings as you close the session.

Suggestions: All join hands in a circle and ask each to finish the statement, "I learned. . . ." Ask several to share one way that they feel they might change their view of male and female roles. Share "I will . . ." statements in relationship to what they learned about sex roles.

Suggested Prayer. Father, help us to see that we are persons with all kinds of feelings, needs, and wants; that we have a variety of skills to be used to help ourselves and others live a more full and creative life. Help us clear our minds of old stereotypes and give us insight to ways we can change in order to be more sensitive persons. Amen.

IF YOU HAVE MORE TIME

Boys—Girls Teach-In

To help teens experience what is meant by a sex role, cross the roles. In order to accomplish this, parents and patient adults may be assistants. Perhaps this is also a way to work in grandparents or senior citizens. Have the youth list sex roles for boys/men and girls/women. Then the group decides which "boy role" and which "girl role" it is going to teach the opposite sex.

Example: Boys may teach girls how a lawn mower works and some techniques for mowing lawns. Girls could give the boys some babysitting tips. (This is assuming that boys could learn more about babysitting and girls don't know about lawn mowing.) You and the group choose the "new learnings" to be taught according to your interests. When the "Teach-In" is over, the girls may choose to get some lawn-mowing jobs, the boys some babysitting jobs, and the donations of the money could go for a charitable cause.

WHY?

New insights and awareness can become more real when we experience them and especially more apt to become practiced if we allow for learning change by practice.

Listening to Lyrics

WHY?

Much money is made yearly by the sale of records, tapes, and tickets to Broadway plays and movies. Youth is one of the biggest audiences of records and tapes. This indicates thousands of people listen over and over to lyrics that stereotype male and female roles, feelings, and behaviors. What we hear and see is how we learn. By listening to songs that were/are popular, we can discover some of the patterns from which we get our sex-role learnings. To become aware is the first step toward change.

MATERIALS NEEDED: Stereo or hi-fi player, depending upon the type of records you are playing.

Records: *Flower Drum Song* by Richard Rodgers and Oscar Hammerstein II, Decca Records DL79098 (available on loan from most public libraries).

South Pacific, Richard Rodgers and Oscar Hammerstein II, RCA Victor LSO-1032 (available on loan from most public libraries).

These suggestions are based specifically on these two musicals of the past. Other records of your choice can be dealt with in the same manner. (Choose those that best fit you and the group hearing them.) It may be helpful to give the group some background about each musical before random listening. This may also shed some light on where the stereotypes are coming from. Information about the musical are on the record jackets. Play the following songs from *Flower Drum*

Song. Some suggested questions are listed to use as guides for reflection.

• "I Enjoy Being a Girl": What female characteristics are mentioned? List them and have the boys mark the ones they agree with and the girls mark the ones they feel are "right on." Compare and allow for cross comparisons and rebuttal. Which ones would each sex group change? Why? Have both sexes list male characteristics and compare those lists the same way.

• "Fan Tan Fanny": This is another look in a different way at "another kind" of female behavior.

• "Don't Marry Me": A young man sings about why a young woman shouldn't marry him. Listen for the male characteristics he sings about. Which ones do you believe are true for you? Which ones do you want to keep for your value system?

• "Gliding Through My Memoree": A male sings about his past girl friends. List the number of female characteristics that are important to him. Then have the boys mark the ones they feel are important to them. Have the girls look at the list and see how they feel about those listed. Which ones would they change?

• "The Other Generation": Adults sing about the younger generation. List all the stereotypes you can hear mentioned. You may need to play this twice or three times. Are there any sex-roles specifically mentioned? What does it have to say about adults? About grandparents? Do you agree with any of the statements in the song? Disagree?

• "The Other Generation (Reprise)": The youth sing about the adults. Listen and see if any of these lyrics sound like youth talking today. Any stereotypes here? Which statements do you agree with? Disagree with?

Play the following from *South Pacific.* Questions are listed to use as guides for listening.

• "There Is Nothin' like a Dame": In this song sailors are singing about women, and they list the things guys "need" dames for. How many can you list? Which ones do you agree with? Disagree? Where besides this song have you heard any of these stereotypes?

• "I'm Gonna Wash That Man Right outa My Hair": What does this song say about relationships between men and women? Is that the way you want to relate to the opposite sex, or have them relate to you?

• "A Wonderful Guy" and "Younger than Spring-time": (Listen to these two before discussing them.) Both of these songs are about love. In "A Wonderful Guy" a girl sings about her feelings and behaviors when she's in love. Does this follow any pattern you have heard or seen anywhere else before? In "Younger Than

Springtime" a boy sings about a girl. How "typical" is this of "young love"?

• "Happy Talk": What does this say about male-female conversations? Do you agree? Would you add anything to the list of happy talk? What does the line in the song mean about needing a dream in order to have a dream come true?

• "Carefully Taught": What does this say about how and when we learn? What does this have to say to us about where, when, and how we learn sex roles and sex stereotypes? As an individual, what roles do you want to keep? Why? Can we change the old patterns if we don't want to live by the stereotypes? Have group members suggest ways to encourage change where they want change.

Have the youth bring in records that are popular today—pop tunes, country western, and show tunes. Following the same type of listening and discussion, see how today's lyrics compare or differ from those of the past.

"Swap Learn"

To help teens experience what other roles "feel" like, perhaps they can become involved in a project that will benefit others at the same time that they learn. One suggestion is to have male and female adults assist in teaching new skills. Example: Boys could learn how to bake batter bread to be used for church Communion. Girls could learn to use tools so they could make a cross for the Communion table. Both sexes could be a part of serving the Communion or a part of the service. Keep in mind that the "normal" jobs for men and women are now to be "swapped" so that learning can take place.

Another project would be for girls to learn enough skills to make a toy(s) out of metal or wood and boys to learn sewing skills to make toys, toss pillows, or bean bags. The toys could then be donated to a children's home, used for special gifts for the needy, for the church nursery, or for the local day-care center.

WHY?

New insights and awarenesses come "alive" when we experience what we have just talked about. We learn best by doing.

Jackie Johnson is a home-economics teacher in Merrill, Wisconsin, and a trainer in personal growth with youth, adults, and family-life groups.

WHAT HAS THIS GOT TO DO WITH DATING?

Friendship is the first step in the courting process

by JACKIE JOHNSON

Basic feelings, emotional and physical needs, inner conflict—we all have these in common. We also all share the need *to learn to love.*

The loving life of every normal person develops in these stages: self-love of the baby, mother love, family love, gang love, adolescent love, and mature love. During the young teen years, persons are learning to know and enjoy the companionship of the opposite sex. Dating in these years is a way to practice and learn the steps that lead toward mature love.

Teens have growing affection for the other sex and are susceptible to "puppy love." Often dating is done to get something from the relationship without thinking of giving. Learning to think of others and getting satisfaction from giving as well as from getting is a step that takes place in the family love stage. Often it has not developed or is not learned, and then adolescents need to be helped to become aware of the importance of thinking of others.

This program is designed to help the young teen take a look at what it is like to manipulate and be manipulated and to discover the methods each uses to get what he or she wants.

PURPOSES

To stimulate feelings of being manipulated in an unthreatening way in order to see what manipulation feels like;

WHY?

Teens often are subtly manipulated but sublimate their feelings because of peer pressure or parental teachings. In this activity they are given a chance to respond to manipulation, compare these feelings to other experiences of manipulation, and deal with those feelings.

To determine if we use different techniques of manipulation with different sexes;

To determine if we want to continue in our patterns of relating or to change.

PROCEDURE

TIME REQUIRED: twenty to thirty minutes for the exercise, ten minutes for discussion.

Step 1

Introduce the exercise. Have persons meet with another person of the same sex and sit on the floor facing each other. Each pair decides which person will begin by placing his or her hands together as if to pray with fingers interlocking. The other person is to unfold his or her partner's fingers to get the hands apart. Each can resist the pulling as much as he or she wants.

Step 2

When the hands have been pulled apart or a period of five minutes has elapsed, have the couple exchange places. The one who "unfolded hands" now folds her or his hands, and the other person "unfolds." When this segment is finished, have each couple spend a few minutes talking about what happened. How did it feel to unfold? To be unfolded? Did one resist more than the other?

Step 3

Have each person find a new partner, this time—of the opposite sex. Repeat the experience with the boy doing the "unfolding" first and then the girl. After both have done the activity, be sure to spend a few minutes talking about what happened to them: how it felt to unfold and to be unfolded. Compare feelings when the exercise was done with a person of the same sex, and with someone of the opposite sex.

Step 4

Have the total group form a close circle. Here are some suggested questions that will help the group discover feelings about the experience:

Look at hands. Whose are the reddest from being pulled? Ask for individuals to share briefly their experience. How did they feel being pulled at? How much did they resist and stay in control? How long did each seem to resist? Did some give up easily? Why?

What, if anything, does this say about how we push or pull others around? How does it feel to manipulate a person? To be manipulated? Were any of these feelings similar to other experiences you've had? Were there different feelings when you were with the opposite sex? Did you use any different methods with the opposite sex than with the same sex? How does this relate to your dealing with the same/opposite sex?

Where in your life are you manipulated? If not physically, then subtly or nonverbally? When or whom do you manipulate? Do you want to change? How can change take place? How does this exercise relate to dating? Have each person share "I learned . . . about me" statements.

IF YOU HAVE MORE TIME

Let's Do It

WHY?

This experience is designed to discover personal behaviors in relating with others while getting what we want. It is important for leaders to be aware of and sensitive to the responses of the youth. Encourage sharing of similar experiences from real life.

MATERIAL NEEDED: slips of paper with a number from 2 to 25 on each; two persons to be observers, preferably adults so all youth have the experience of being in the game.

TIME REQUIRED: 30–45 minutes

Introduce the game by saying, "This game will help to determine what we do in the next half hour." Each person is given a slip of paper *which only he or she is to see, until he or she chooses to give it up.* Each is asked to think a minute about what activity he or she wants to do in the next half hour. Then each is to go around to

persons and "convince" others to do this activity with them. When one has convinced another, both yell, "Let's Do It!" Both stay together and continue to convince others to do that activity. The slips of paper are given to the "convincer" and added to his or her score.

Unannounced Rules. (These rules may be talked about after the game is over.)

A small group can do anything it wants with its score.

The group may still want to do an activity of its choice. Allow for this if time permits.

Procedure

Play the game for fifteen to thirty minutes, depending upon the interest and activity of the group. When time is called, add up each person's score. Who has the most points?

Have group participants sit in a circle and share what happened. Some questions to get at the meaning of the experience for the participants are:

What happened? Whom did you try to convince? Why? How did you feel trying to talk someone into doing your thing? How did you feel being talked to? What thoughts were going through your mind as you convinced/were convincing? Does having a high or low score say anything to you?

How "real" is this activity in terms of your own experiences? Do you relate to people this way when you want something? Are you aware that the game itself is subtle manipulation? Did you experience any feelings you have had in real life? How do they compare? Share those experiences. Is all manipulation "bad"? Cite some cases where it may be "good."

Have the observers share what they saw without judging behaviors. They are the TV cameras, not the judge. Others may be able to "chime in" and share, too. Ask each person what he or she learned about himself/herself in relating to others? Do you want to keep relating like you did in the game? Do you want to relate this way in dating experiences? If not, how can you change?

Looking at the Scriptures

Here are some Bible selections that can be used to explore meanings; that may shed light on the previous exercises.

1 John 4:7-8— Let us love one another.

Ephesians 4:25— Speak the truth with your neighbor—members together.

1 John 4:20-21— He who loves God should love his brother.

1 John 4:11— We should love one another.

1 Timothy 4:12-16—Do not let anyone look down on you because you are young.

Colossians 2:8— See that no one makes a captive of you.

Philippians 4:8— Fill your mind with those things that are good.

Romans 6:16— When you surrender as slaves to someone—you are a slave.

Romans 14:19— Aim at those things that bring peace.

Luke 6:31— Do unto others as you would have them do unto you.

Acts 20:35— It is more blessed to give than receive.

Leviticus 19:13— Do not oppress your neighbor.

Leviticus 19:18— Love your neighbor as yourself.

John 13:34-35— Commandment to love one another.

What do these Scriptures have to say about our relating to other persons, especially in dating?

In Closing

(Have copies of this reading available for each person.)

Divide into two groups, each responding to the other:

Group

1: I want friends—and I need to love someone and to be loved by them.
2: A *real* friendship is a rare thing today.
1: I am conscious of so many reasons not to trust others.
2: A real friendship is half my responsibility.
1: So often I have tried to be free, to relate, to be open and honest with others, and they have merely gone about their business or changed the subject, or suggested we do something else. So often I have tried to give myself to the other person, only to be tolerated. And that's worse than nothing.
2: I've tried winning friends by doing the other person's thing instead of telling them what I really wanted in our friendship.
1: I'm not a number, a thing, a rock.
2: I do not want to be counted, added, graded, handled, manipulated.

1: I love, I fear, I laugh, I cry—I have feelings.
2: I love, I fear, I laugh, I cry—I have feelings.
1: And I want to share with you, and you!
2: And I want to share with you, and you!
1: —But you came back at me with the weather or the ball game or something else—anything else as long as it was not something close, inside, where everything is personal and full of life and meaning.
2: A real friendship is a rare thing today—and half of the responsibility is mine.
1: I want to care about people and be cared about— not used and manipulated.
2: I want to care about people and be cared about— not used and manipulated.
1: You talk—but not with me.
2: You talk—but not with me.
1: You touch—but it could be anybody.
2: I try to reach out and be myself with you—to give you something of me that's rich and meaningful. And you go right on talking as if I were not there.
1: I meet a person and I want to be met as a person— to be treated as a person.
2: I want to meet each person and be treated as a person.
1: But can I trust him? Can I trust her? I've been let down so many times.
2: Won't this just be one more passing affair—only temporary? I don't know, I don't know.
1: I want to love and care about someone and to be loved and cared about by her. I take the risk.
2: I trust myself to this person and he accepts me in openness—no using—no manipulation—just freedom to relate.
1: I can trust myself with this person—in openness—no using—only freedom to be myself without manipulation.
2: We share—we talk with each other.
1: We talk—together.
2: A friendship is half my responsibility.

ALL: A *real* friendship is a rare thing today—worth every risk I take to be myself with another person.

QUICKIE FOLLOW-UP ACTIVITIES

WHY?

To do activities that help us practice what we verbalize helps the learning "sink in" deeper.

---

1. Play the record "I Gotta Be Me" and listen to the words. Respond to:

    How can I be me and still allow for others in my life? Such as my family? My date?

2. Brainstorm kinds of places to go as a date that would be fun for both persons. Both can be winners; no one needs to lose!

3. Have a poster session. Using pictures from magazines, drawings, color or marking pens, illustrate the poster saying of your choice. (Choose a Bible verse, a line from a poem, or your own thought as the "saying" for the poster.) Choose one of these or make up your own. These could be used as a part of a service or to "decorate" the youth room.

Jackie Johnson is a home-economics teacher and a trainer in personal growth with youth, adults, and family-life groups.

ALCOHOL— WHAT SHALL WE DO WITH IT?

Results of the use of alcohol

by ROGER C. PALMS

GOAL

To discover ways that alcohol hurts, and the real needs of drinking people.

PROCEDURE

Step 1

As the session begins, divide into two groups and talk about the following two cases:

Case 1. A girl in junior high has friends who want her to drink with them. She refuses. They think she is refusing because she is afraid to try. They laugh at her. She doesn't tell them the real reason. Most evenings when she goes home, she finds her mother drunk. If you were that girl, what would you do?

Case 2. When others in school get new clothes, Bob is still wearing the same stuff he wore a couple of years ago. Some of the guys mock him. They tell him he hasn't any style, he doesn't know what's in, and Bob says nothing. Bob has a father who spends his paycheck on alcohol. There isn't any money left for clothes. If you were Bob, what would you do?

Step 2

Now, ask the small groups if they know some other case or cases. After some thought they could present them to the others in the group through role playing. Remember not to disclose the identity of others. *Caution:* Alcoholism is not the only problem with the

---

WHY?

The more we see the emotional involvement and the innocent victims, the more we realize that alcohol is not just a pleasure or life-style problem.

---

use of alcohol. There are special problems related to teens themselves drinking. Encourage the group to describe these. (Examples: lack of moderation of teens, interference with study, problems with the law.)

Step 3

Having thought about the results of alcohol in these two lives and the lives of the persons they role-played, ask each group member to write on the chalkboard or newsprint other effects or results of alcohol. Get as many as you can. Look at the long-range effects (i.e., the grain used that might feed starving people, traffic accidents, higher insurance for us all, effects on a community, extra police protection, higher taxes, etc.).

For those in the group willing to do some advanced study, ask them this week to contact their council of churches, city government offices, or library to find out how much alcohol is specifically costing their community or city in dollars, jobs, and lives. Reports can be presented next session.

WHY?

Junior highs need to understand that the argument "drinking is a personal thing that involves me only" is nonsense. What we do with alcohol affects ourselves, our families, our community, even the rest of the nation or world.

Step 4

What people say about alcohol or what the magazine ads declare about alcohol is different from what we see around us. What are some of the tantalizing statements made about alcohol? If you believe what you hear or read, "Alcohol will . . ." (ask each one to complete the sentence on a piece of paper).

Now look at what the Bible says (Proverbs 23:29-35).

Using your sentence "Alcohol will . . .", change the word "alcohol" to Jesus Christ. Complete the sentence "Jesus Christ will. . . ."

What does this say about human need? Alcohol is a substitute for what people really crave.

For those who want to do extra work, suggest they talk to the pastor about the needs of people and the way alcohol is used as a substitute for Jesus Christ to "satisfy" those needs. The pastor may even be able to suggest books on the subject of personal needs.

Step 5

What are the basic differences between what alcohol offers and what Jesus offers? (Example: one brings life; the other destroys life; one gives happiness, the other gives misery, etc.) These differences can be listed on shirt boards, poster board, or on a graffiti board, and taped anywhere in the room.

Step 6

To continue affirming ourselves, our needs, and above all, the One who supplies those needs, add to the collection just taped to the walls the sentences done in Step 4, "Jesus Christ will. . . ." You might even color them or add art work or borders.

Leave them up for several weeks to remind yourselves and others that Jesus Christ is all sufficient.

Close the session with prayer, asking people to pray not only for themselves but also for friends whom they know are already moving toward alcoholism. Pray for a way to steer them from this, by meeting the needs that are "driving them to drink."

POSSIBLE PROJECTS

For those who may wish to do additional work this week, consider the following:

1. Visit a halfway house for alcoholics in your city if there is one. Talk to the director and preferably some of the residents. Find out how they got started using alcohol. How do their fellow residents keep them from going back to drink?

2. Ask a social worker, your pastor, or a school counselor if there are statistics available on the number of men/women alcoholics. Why do men drink? Why do women drink? How can you teach the reasons to classmates and group members to help them avoid the pitfalls?

3. Find out through the library how much grain goes into the production of alcohol. How many people in the world could be kept from starving to death if they had that grain?

Even if only one person in the group does any of these projects, it will influence future programs. If no one does them, group participants will still reflect on this program the next time they hear about alcohol breaking up a home or read newspaper articles about starvation in the world.

Roger C. Palms is editor of <u>Decision</u> magazine and the author of <u>The Jesus Kids</u> and <u>The Christian and the Occult.</u>

WHAT ABOUT SMOKING?

Why teens begin smoking—and why not to

by ROGER C. PALMS

GOAL

To consider the personal implications of smoking.

PROCEDURE

Step 1: The Conflict

As the session begins, ask two groups to form, one to present the positive reasons for smoking and the second group to present the negative reasons.

Ask the first group to come up with a "sales pitch" to present the "positive" view to the other group. They can use ads from magazines or newspapers that are just brought in and dumped on the floor, or draw on any other information about tobacco which the people in the groups have.

For example: "Be sophisticated"; "Be a real man"; "Why not be a lady and be offered . . . ?", etc.

Give them time to prepare the sales pitch and then select a "salesperson." The only rule for the salesperson is that he or she does not use the word "tobacco." This forces the salesperson to search for words to describe his or her product rather than just settling for a name.

The second group is to come up with the negative aspect of smoking, such as, "It will take away your taste for food; perhaps it will give you cancer; it stains

---

WHY?

Only when group members have a chance to probe their own thoughts about the use of tobacco, will they realize that they are being handed a sales pitch every time they pick up a newspaper or magazine. They are being sold something, and it will be evident that what they are being sold can be destructive to them and the people they love.

---

the walls of your room;" etc. This salesperson should avoid using the word "tobacco" also.

When they are ready, have the two salespersons present their pitches to the entire group.

For those who would like to do additional work: Ask them to contact the advertising department of their newspaper and ask why they accept ads for a destructive drug. List the answers given and share them with the group next time. They might also prepare a letter to the editor of the same paper listing the reasons given by the advertising department to see if they will print it.

Step 2: Some Tough Questions

Group members can move around the room as the following questions are asked. In fact, a game can be made of it. Ask a question; let the group mix as they talk over the answer. Give two or three minutes; then say, "Freeze!" As they stop where they are, choose someone to tell the responses he or she heard in his or her conversations.

Then ask the next question and let them wander around discussing it again, choosing a different person to report when you say, "Freeze!"

QUESTIONS

1. Cigarette, pipe, and cigar companies spend millions of dollars in advertising to sell their products, yet the surgeon general insists that smoking may be killing people. Is tobacco really a harmless pleasure? Is it a dangerous drug?

2. What other sources of information are there where truth can be discovered about tobacco?

3. What do people who smoke or have stopped smoking say about tobacco?

4. What does your doctor say about the use of tobacco?

5. What do your friends at school say about tobacco?

6. What does the Bible say about treating the body with respect?

WHY?

Obviously, because there are as many views and opinions as there are people, there has to be a source other than the emotional feelings of human beings in order to learn something concrete about smoking. Human reason or health arguments don't really make any difference when we are dealing with emotional choices.

Step 3: A New Dimension

What does the Bible say about smoking? Write on the chalkboard two "verses":

1. "Thou shalt not use tobacco."

2. "Take a little tobacco for your health's sake."

Hand out Bibles and ask the group members if they can find these "passages" in the Scripture.

When they agree that these are not Bible verses, ask them what the Bible does say:

1. about the body as the temple of God;

2. about presenting our bodies as a living sacrifice, holy and acceptable;

3. about remaining pure, spotless.

Bibles with a concordance will help the group members find these passages. They could pair up and search for these as teams.

WHY?

Obviously the Bible does not use the word "tobacco" or say anything about it anywhere. Any discoveries in Scripture about tobacco have to come from a different direction.

Ask the group to decide if the passages of Scripture found do apply to the use of tobacco. If so, why? Did they discover other passages?

For those willing to go further with this, a sermon or teaching message can be prepared on the body as the temple of God, and permission can be secured to present it to the congregation some Sunday. It would make a real impact on the adults and young people who are present.

Step 4: An Unhooked Life-Style

Give group members a sheet of paper and a pencil and ask them to write out their own theology or covenant or standard in regard to tobacco.

Ask several to read to the group the statements they have written.

Then, standing in a circle, ask each to pray audibly or silently for the person on the right that he or she will be able to carry out the covenant.

Roger C. Palms is editor of <u>Decision</u> magazine and the author of <u>The Jesus Kids</u> and <u>The Christian and the Occult.</u>

DRUGS: FRIEND OR ENEMY?

Some personal needs that lead to drug abuse

by ROGER C. PALMS

GOAL

To help persons explore the dangers in using hard drugs and to discover some of the reasons that people use drugs.

PROCEDURE

Step 1: Names of Drugs

As group participants gather, ask them to brainstorm as quickly as possible to compose a list of drugs they know about which young people are using. They can list them on newsprint or a chalkboard. Then, when the list is made, go down the list asking, "Are any of these safe?" Some may list marijuana or a few other "safe" drugs.

On a scale beginning with one for the least dangerous and going up to the most dangerous, ask the group to put in order the drugs that are listed. Do it first individually on separate sheets of paper; then put them corporately on the board. Are there arguments? Do all agree? (You may need to list standards for "safety," such as danger of addiction.)

Be alert to arguments coming out. The wise counselor begins to pick up statements from individuals that call for personal conversation later in the week.

Step 2: Am I a Likely Candidate for Drugs?

> **WHY?**
>
> Drug addicts aren't born; they become addicts for varied reasons. We all could come to depend on drugs unless we recognize weaknesses and compensate. The following exercise will help to alert the group to causes of addiction and head off any drift into drugs that can so easily occur.

Pass out sheets of paper. Let the group members make out a personal checklist.
1. Do I have a need to escape?
2. Do I look for easy solutions?
3. Do I find pain difficult to endure?
4. Do I like quick solutions to difficult situations?
5. How well do I "grin and bear it"?

> **WHY?**
>
> Studies show that people who take drugs have a low pain level. They are escapists who do not know how to handle difficulties. They need drugs. Logic won't stop people from using drugs. Even those who have come off heroin through hospital or jail will often go back on, some even for the addiction to the needle more than anything else. They have a psychological need for it.

For those willing to do extra study: Ask them to talk to doctors or social workers or school counselors about the reasons people go back on drugs once they are "clean." The answers could be very revealing and worth sharing with the total group.

Step 3: How do People Get Started?

Besides the psychological need, what other influences make people either start or continue drugs?

Ask the group to talk about the various reasons that people start on drugs: a pusher at school, pressure of friends, or the idea of trying something new.

Now comes the hard part. Ask if several would share an experience they had in which someone tried to get them to try drugs. Ask which pressures are the hardest to overcome. Ask how they can help one another withstand that pressure.

Can anyone in the group share an experience with a

friend (avoid using names) in which he or she tried to persuade the friend to stay away from drugs? Ask this person to tell about it. Maybe there are several experiences among the group members.

WHY?

Many junior highs know people who are drug users. They tend either to keep quiet about it or only discuss it with close friends. As a result it's not a subject that comes into their "Christian" conversations. Open talk in their Christian fellowship is very healthy. It also creates a group feeling so that, having discussed it once, they will not be as hesitant about bringing it up again when temptations come.

For those wanting to do additional work: Suggest planning a drug counseling time at the church. What might be the results? Could they use adults, college students? Their "fact finding" can help the group decide if this is a program that it wants to undertake.

Step 4: Being the Body of Believers

Using Ephesians 4, 1 Corinthians 12, and 1 Peter 4 for reference, what does the Bible say about the body of Christ? What does it say about ministering to each other? What does it say about helping one another discover who we are? If a person really got hold of this, would he or she use drugs?

Step 5: Deprogramming

Divide into groups of three and ask each group to come up with a one-minute radio or television "deprogramming" commercial. These television or radio "spots" must be specific and to the point. Junior highs are good at this. These can be fun to do using situation humor or even scare tactics.

In their "spots," be sure they have thought out what it is that they are saying to their friends or to adults about how to get off drugs, or why they should get off drugs. This collection of "spots" might later be presented to other groups in the church, even down to the kindergarten level.

Step 6: Never Start

The best way to avoid drugs is never to begin. Ask the members to join hands and pray that those in their group will never start with drugs. Then reassure them that if they do start or even play a little bit with drugs now, they have a family here which cares about them.

Roger C. Palms is editor of Decision magazine and the author of The Jesus Kids and The Christian and the Occult.

I HAVE FEELINGS

Looking at feelings that are hard to handle

by VIRGINIA S. RICH

Junior highs are just beginning to be aware of their feelings of sexuality. Sometimes they are frightened by these feelings which are new and strange and hard to handle. Sometimes they repress them or go overboard in flaunting them. They almost always find it difficult to talk about them. These art experiences should help them get their feelings out where they can look at them and talk about them and see them as good, God-given, and human. This should enable them to handle these feelings in a mature way.

PEOPLE LANDSCAPES

> ### WHY?
>
> Our bodies express our sexuality; life-sized portrayals of our bodies are one way to share these expressions with the group.

Materials

two sheets of body-sized paper for each person
(use a roll of brown wrapping paper, newsprint
roll-ends, table-cover paper, or newspaper sheets
  taped together)
scissors
felt-tip markers
poster paint
fabric scraps, yarn, collage-type materials
glue
stapler and staples
newspaper
record player and records

PROCEDURE

1. Have an area where the paper can be laid out and another area in which everyone can move around.
2. Play music and have the group move around to the rhythm. One way to do this may be to suggest that participants close their eyes, listen to the music, and, staying in one place, move their bodies to what the music suggests. Or, if there is a lot of space available, the group can move around freely in the room.

3. When members of the group are ready, each one will lie down on one of the body-sized papers and arrange his or her body in a position which the music and the movement have suggested. Have several people available to draw around each person on the paper. Continue music until everyone has been drawn.

4. Make available the paint, markers, glue, scissors, and collage materials, and let each person decorate his/her paper figure to express how he/she felt while moving to the music.

5. Cut out the decorated figure along with a second piece of paper so that there will be two identical paper figures.

Staple the two layers of paper together, leaving a good-sized opening.

7. Stuff rumpled-up newspaper into the stapled figure to give a three-dimensional look.

8. When all figures are finished, encourage each person to tell why he/she decorated the figure in that manner. Did he/she feel good about the music and movement? Did he/she feel self-conscious? How did participants' feelings affect how they decorated the paper figure? How do they feel about themselves as young women or young men?

9. Hang each figure from the wall or ceiling with masking tape or string to make a large group landscape.

ME BOXES

> ### WHY?
>
> This is a three-dimensional way to express individuality.

Materials

A variety of large cardboard boxes
Poster paint and/or latex paint
Colored construction paper
Cardboard scraps
Fabric scraps, yarn, string
Small wood scraps
Magazines, newspapers
Scissors
Glue
Stapler and staples

Procedure

1. All sides of the box are to be decorated in a way that will say something personal about the one who made the box.

2. Some may decorate just the inside of the box, some just the outside. Some may want to make each side of the box portray a different aspect of life, such as school, hobby, family, friends, likes and dislikes, or sports. Some may want to build secret compartments or cut windows in the box. Some may use words and letters cut from magazines.

3. When boxes are finished, give each person time to tell why he/she chose to decorate it in that particular way. Display the boxes by hanging them from the ceiling or tacking them on a bulletin board.

ADVERTISING CAMPAIGN

WHY?

Use magazine ads to do some thinking about what images of sexuality they give us.

Materials

A variety of old magazines
Scissors
Rubber erasers
Felt-tip markers
Glue

Procedure

1. Have the group look at a number of magazine ads. Discuss how they try to make you think about your sexual image.

2. After discussing the images advertisements try to give us, think and talk about how the group members would like to change the ads to give a different sexual image.

3. Each person can make up a new advertisement for a real product. Take an ad and, using an eraser, remove parts of the print and replace these areas with different words and designs using felt-tip markers. Or, cut up several different ads and glue them back together to make a new one.

4. If someone comes up with a good idea for an advertisement, make a large copy of it to put up like a small billboard.

5. Try looking at and changing television commercials the same way.

SYMBOLIC PATCHWORK

WHY?

An activity to encourage thought about a personal trait or interest which could be symbolic of an individual.

Materials

One 12″ square of plain fabric per person (use muslin or pieces of an old sheet)
A variety of fabric scraps
Yarn, rickrack, buttons, etc.
Needles
Thread
Glue
Scissors

Procedure

1. Talk about symbols, trademarks, signs, and how they convey information in a concise way. Having some examples to show would be helpful. Discuss what kind of symbol or picture or design could express who a person is. The symbols might depict a skill, a hobby, a favorite piece of clothing, an organization, a sport, or whatever will identify a particular person.

2. Have each person design such a symbol on paper. Keep the designs simple. Omit all unnecessary details.

3. Make the symbol with the scraps available, using a 12″ square as a background for the design. The pieces can be sewed or glued onto the background.

4. Sew the pieces together to make a patchwork wall hanging. After several weeks see how many can remember who made which patch.

Virginia S. Rich is an artist and churchwoman from Devon, Pennsylvania.

SELF-EXPRESSION THROUGH CREATIVE ARTS

Who am I? and Who are you?

by JOELLEN BOWER

"Who am I?" and "Who are you?" are two of the most important questions young teens ask. One of the best ways of finding answers to these questions is through creative art. And teens don't have to be artists or even artistic to do this. When self-expression is the goal, the meaning of the creation is more important than how "well" it is done.

PERSONALIZED NAMETAGS

WHY?

This activity will help youth in a new group to get acquainted with one another and to discover more than simply one another's names.

Materials

Construction paper
Scissors
Felt-tip pens
Straight or safety pins

Procedure

Let each person in the group (you, too) make his/her own name tag, showing by the shape of the tag or by its decoration various activities or interests. For instance, a musician might cut a name tag in the shape of a musical instrument. Later, the tags could be hung around the room for decoration. This activity would be ideal for a first meeting and would lend some interest to the get-acquainted process, which can be awkward. It could also be used during a joint meeting of two or more groups.

COLLAGES

Materials

Old magazines
Scissors
Paste
Large sheets of paper

WHY?

Making collages allows youth to express their interests and concerns, and to discover and appreciate diversity in others.

Procedure

Ask the members of your group to join you in sitting around a large table, with a large sheet of paper in front of each one. Invite them to go through the old magazines and cut out any pictures or words which describe who they are, what their interests and concerns consist of, the type of humor they like, their "favorite things," a landscape they would like to live in, etc. Afterward, they can arrange what they have found on their paper in any way they choose, making it a collage.

Then invite each person to show what she or he has created, and explain why each item on the collage was included. Be sure to do one yourself and share it. Through exchange and discussion, the differences and similarities in the group become immediately evident and can be built upon in future sessions.

This activity could be used almost anywhere in a program schedule—as a kick-off point, a "midway" method to take stock of where they all are and how they are feeling, or as a final activity to wrap up the year with an exercise in self-affirmation.

SERENDIPITY SESSION

Materials

Writing materials

59

Paints
Newsprint
Construction paper
Old magazines
Crayons
Any scrap material which may be available

WHY?

This experience gives persons a chance to express themselves through the media of their choice, and to gain appreciation for ways in which others express themselves.

Procedure

Invite members of the group to express themselves through one or more of the materials available. For instance, suggest that they use a most imaginative way of expressing one or two very important ideas. When the project is completed (it can take up more than one meeting, if desired), have each person discuss his or her creation and share it with the others. The "creations" can become permanent decorations for the meeting room.

This exercise could be part of an effort to make the room a group "place," or it could fit into a larger program dealing with the arts or personal values.

SLIDE (OR PHOTO) STORY

WHY?

A slide or photographic story can visually demonstrate who each person is, as an individual and as a family member.

Materials

Slide projector and screen
Large cardboard pieces
Mounting corners for photographs
A large table

Procedure

Ask each person to bring in several slides, photographs, or mementos, some of which demonstrate who *they* are and some of which illustrate who they are as part of a family unit. At the next meeting, have each person show what he or she has brought. Let the youth figure out how to put all the slides, etc., together into a

group portrait which expresses the different roles the members of the group play. They may decide to put all the individual pictures together and all the family shots separately, or to mix them. If they wish to pursue and develop a personal media expression, they could add music or develop their own script and present the project to a church meeting in order to share their identities as persons and as a group. This activity could also be a creative addition to a series on family life.

HANG-UPS

WHY?

This activity is a relatively nonthreatening way to express and explore negative aspects of identity, in the form of "hang-ups."

Materials

Wire coat hangers
Old magazines
Construction paper
Magic Markers
String
Scissors

Procedure

Invite students to illustrate one or more "hang-ups," either by cutting pictures out of the magazines and pasting them on small sheets of paper or by drawing or writing on the construction paper. Each person suspends the pieces of paper from a coat hanger and shows it to the group. (You will want to do this activity, too.) A discussion about hang-ups and what can be done about them can easily take place during or after the activity. This graphic expression of one aspect of self could fit very well into a series on identity, values, etc.

PERSONAL BANNERS

WHY?

This activity gives youth a chance to express what is important in several different areas in their lives. It is also a way of affirming "who I am."

Materials

Large sheets of paper, or pieces of burlap

Old magazines, felt scraps, construction paper
Scissors
Magic Markers
Any available scrap material

Procedure

Suggest that the youth divide their pieces of paper or burlap into six sections. For an especially creative group, let each of them choose six important areas in their lives and illustrate each. Or, you might suggest some categories yourself, such as:

1. favorite hobby or activity
2. fondest wish or dream
3. favorite family activity
4. what is liked best in school (which subject, activity, etc.)
5. greatest personal achievement
6. what you would do if you had one year to live and were assured of success in whatever you chose to do.

Invite them to illustrate these different aspects in any way they like, but encourage pictures and symbols over words. Feel free to use your imagination in creating categories that might represent particular concerns in your group.

This activity would be particularly useful in a series having to do with personality and/or identity. It could also be modified in such a way that the focus would be on issues believed important by the youth. Each person could portray one or more issues of concern and some possible solutions to the problem(s). Although this activity is not specifically expressive of identity, it is related, for in many ways people are what they believe. Developing values and priorities and an attitude toward pressing concerns of our day is an important part of discovering personal identity.

JoEllen Bower is a student at Kalamazoo College and formerly was an editorial interne in the Department of Ministry with Youth, American Baptist Churches in the U.S.A.

A DRAMA ABOUT DRUGS

Junior highs produce their own drama
to teach younger children about drugs

by ROGER C. PALMS

Because younger children idolize and like to follow teenagers, there is both a responsibility and an opportunity to teach them about drugs. Your junior high group can develop an original play to do this.

Ask the pastor or church school leaders for an opportunity sometime during the next month to present the play. Perhaps you will be able to present it in each class or during an evening service.

GETTING STARTED

Call for a weekend (Friday evening through Saturday noon) to plan, write, and rehearse a play about drugs.

Remember to pray for the audiences who will be seeing the play.

Writing the Script

Call the group together to determine a theme or situation for the play. Will it be a hospital emergency room, a family living room, a school corridor? Now you have content, time, and the vehicle or situation to carry the message.

Then sit on the floor or at work tables, with paper and pencils. In the right-hand column of the paper, have the group outline the content of the play (i.e., what material must be covered). Then let the group chart the time sequences of the play along the left-hand side of the page. They need to estimate the number of minutes for each scene or act. The maximum length of the play should probably be less than fifteen minutes lest it get laborious and lose the exciting quality it must carry.

Break Time

Now that you know where you are going, it is time to break for games and pizza.

Back to Work

With outline, time slots, and material to be covered in hand, the group can build the play. Young people are resourceful; they will know what dialogue communicates and what is just silly. Stay away from cumbersome sets and props. The viewers' imagination can supply those.

Before long, the script, scenes, and any changes will all have been woven in. The play, in its rough form, is finished.

A good night's sleep and breakfast is ahead.

Saturday Morning

Between breakfast and noon dismissal, group participants will be able to rehearse their play. Roles will be assigned by consensus and lines changed some as the play moves along. Everyone should have a part. If background music or a song is part of the play, that can be woven in, too. If the play involves audience participation, that should be part of the practice. The group should know what it expects the audience to do and plan for it.

Before dismissal, agree on the next practice meeting, clean up the kitchen and any litter left in the church, then pray for the play's effective presentation.

EVALUATION

After the play has been presented, meet again to discuss the results. Was it an enjoyable experience? Would the group like to do this again? Did the message get across? How do you know? What feedback came from those who saw the play? What evidence is there that learning took place?

If it was a good experience, you might want to contact a sister church, asking if its congregation would like to see the play.

ALTERNATE GROUP PROJECT

As a group, make plans to visit an alcohol treatment center, a drug rehabilitation center, or a hospital alcohol or drug treatment ward.

Ask for a presentation ahead of time on what happens there so that the extent of the treatment program will be felt.

Prior to the visit, invite a doctor, nurse, police officer, or hospital chaplain to talk to your group.

For further information on drugs, ask the group if it would like to write to the U.S. Senate for the record of hearings. (Marihuana-Hashish Epidemic and Its Impact on United States Security. Hearings before the Sub-Committee to Investigate the Administration of the Internal Security Act and Other Internal Security Laws of the Committee on the Judiciary, United States Senate, Ninety-Third Congress, Second Session, May 9, 16, 17, 21, and June 13, 1974.)

When the record comes, ask several volunteers to give reports on what they read.

Roger C. Palms is editor of <u>Decision</u> magazine and the author of <u>The Jesus Kids</u> and <u>The Christian and the Occult.</u>

CAMP OUT—IN

A retreat focusing on sharing identities

by SHARON BALLENGER

PREPARATION

Step 1

Secure an okay from the church board (trustees, diaconate) before proceeding. Assure them there will be adequate adult supervision and that the church will be back in order before you leave. (Have one or two junior high youth attend this meeting and have them present the request if appropriate.)

Step 2

Permission slips from parents are not a bad idea. You, as a leader, will have the assurance that parents know their kids are spending the night away from home.

Step 3

Meet with a small group of young people and plan. This planning would include food, money, sleeping gear, rules, etc.

Example: $1.00 per person to help defray cost of breakfast; each person bring a snack to share, sleeping bags, guitars, etc. If the youth ministry budget is low, a decision might be made to have different parents furnish supplies for the late night meal, such as sloppy-joe mixture, buns, potato chips, and pop!

Have a "reach out" committee to advertise the camp in. Announcements in the weekly church newsletter and bulletin, plus an announcement during the worship service the Sunday preceding, are suggested!

PROGRAMMING FOR A CAMP IN!

Junior highs like action and variety!
>They like programming done for them!
>>Lots of structure on retreats cuts down on the chaos!
>>>Just be flexible enough to allow more time or less for
>>>>planned ACTIVITIES!
>>Keep discussion periods SHORT!

Step 1

7:00–7:30 P.M.—Sign in! Take money and have them deposit sleeping gear in sleeping area.

7:30–8:00—Then go off to the youth room or meeting area where they are given Magic Markers and construction paper and told to make creative name tags which, hopefully, will say something about who they are!

Sit together in a circle on the floor and share their name tags, adding a little bit about themselves.

HOLD IT!

Leaders may, at this time, use the next few minutes to explain the ground rules:

Example: 1. No phone calls.
2. No leaving the building.
3. Important to stay in your group throughout the evening.
4. No new bodies allowed in at the last minute or during the evening!

DON'T BE AFRAID TO

MAKE THESE RULES AND

ENFORCE THEM!

JUNIOR HIGHS EXPECT AND NEED TO KNOW THE BOUNDARIES!

Step 2

Divide the large group until there are seven to ten in each small group (at least one leader per group).

8:00–9:00—Activity with a focus on self-identity! Materials needed: Lots of butcher paper and/or newsprint, Magic Markers, scissors, and magazines.

Draw human silhouettes! Have each group member lie on the paper and have another member outline his or her body with a Magic Marker. Cut pictures, words, products, etc., from magazines and make a collage on the silhouette telling who you are without naming yourself.

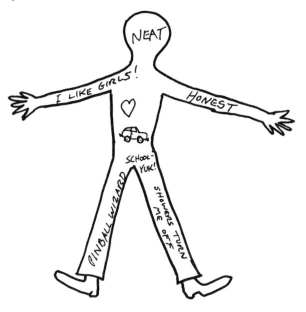

Use masking tape to place silhouettes on wall. Encourage group members to check out the pictures before sitting down to discuss their masterpieces! Sit and talk about the silhouettes. Have group members question one another about different words or pictures which seem unusual.

WHY?

This activity gives leaders clues as to how group members see themselves. Their likes, dislikes, hurts, joys, and values are evident in activities such as this one and can be helpful as leaders decide on future program topics!

BESIDES! IT'S JUST A GOOD IDEA TO BEGIN TO GET PRETTY SPECIFIC ABOUT HOW YOU SEE YOURSELF AND TO SHARE SUCH INSIGHTS WITH OTHERS!

Step 3

9:00–9:30—Snack break. Ping-Pong and volleyball, if available, are fast, energy-expending games between sessions!

Step 4

9:30–10:30—Activity Two: *Self-Disclosure Through Role Play.* Materials: Enough pencils and paper for each person to use!

Have the group divide into threes. This can be done by numbering off. The leader(s) presents several incomplete fantasy situations.(These are stories which are not true but could happen.) Each group member is to write out as briefly as possible how he or she would have ended each of the stories.

Following this, have all the triads share informally how they would have ended the stories. Then, encourage each group of three to take one of the stories, assign characters, and "play it" for the total group.

FANTASY SITUATIONS

1. A classmate at school is also your locker mate. This person takes more than his/her half of the space, and wow! Is it ever a mess! Leftover smelly food, dirty sneakers, and paper wads litter the locker. Today as you open your locker, you find half of a rotting orange dripping on your carefully prepared social studies report. Your locker mate approaches the locker just as you bend down to salvage your hard work. What happens? What do you say?

2. A new student starts school in the middle of the semester. This person is quiet and appears unfriendly. One day, when you enter the cafeteria, you notice the new student sitting alone. What do you do? What happens?

3. You are on your way out of the house to attend a class party. Your mom says she needs to talk with you before you leave. She then announces that she is going

to have a baby in the spring. How do you feel? What do you say?

4. A young teacher (one of your favorites) has just lost his wife and child in a terrible car accident. Shortly after he has returned to school, you meet him coming down the hall. What is your reaction? What do you say?

WHY?

A good way to find out about oneself is to "check out" how you behave when an uncomfortable and/or surprising situation presents itself.

Step 5

10:30–11:00—Wrap up for the evening.

LEADER: Tonight we have explored some activities which might have given us some ideas about who we are. Maybe this evening has not only helped you share who you are with other people, but also you may have discovered one new idea about yourself. For the next few minutes, take a Magic Marker and on the paper around your silhouette write a word or draw a picture depicting what you have learned about yourself tonight.

When they return to the group, have a friendship circle and close with a prayer concerning being glad for who and what we are.

Step 6

11:00—Share a meal together. Clean up the kitchen. Volleyball, talking in small groups, or Ping-Pong playing is a good way for leaders and kids to interact in friendly, informal ways until time to move to the sleep area.

Step 7

3:00 A.M.—Everyone should be ready to be tucked in and settled down for the duration of the early morning hours. You can always hope!

Step 8

8:00–10:00—Have kids prepare breakfast . . . with adult supervision if needed.

Clean up all rooms used. Leaders inspect areas to be sure everything is intact.

Step 9

10:00–10:45—Assemble in meeting area.

Short discussion on the things they liked best about the retreat and the things they liked least.

Step 10

"Tying it all together."

MATERIALS NEEDED: Bibles, balls of string or yarn for each person, Magic Markers, one large sheet of newsprint.

Have someone read Psalm 139—God is always with us; he knows us; and he cares!

LEADER: Having found out some things about yourself, you have also had opportunity during the retreat to find out some things about other people. At this time, I'd like for you to take a Magic Marker and put your name on your silhouette. Then go around the room and look at the different drawings and write a statement on someone else's silhouette telling that person something you found out about him/her as a result of the self-awareness activities the evening before. You might want to do this on several pictures. If you'd like, mention a certain strength that person has or give the person a "goodbye-for-now message."

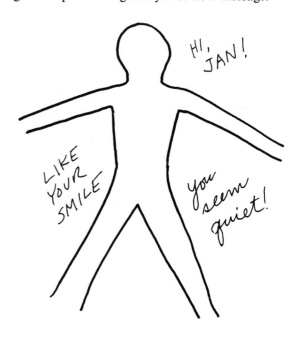

66

Step 11

Back in the total group, give persons an opportunity to thank God for the experience. Then, give them an opportunity to thank each other for this time together.

Step 12

Give each person a Magic Marker, and on the large newsprint have each write a "thank you" to the church for permission to use the building and for their love and trust. (This can be shared in the morning worship service following the retreat!)

Step 13

Give each person a ball of string. Stand in a circle and have each one throw the ball of string across the room to another person, while holding onto the end of the string. Continue to throw string but hang onto some! There should be a maze of string in the middle. Each person is to break off the end of string he or she has and keep it. (This symbolizes tying things together, our relationships together during this time, and keeping a part of what we've had and carrying it home with us!)

RESOURCES FOR RETREATS

Ideas. Edited by Mike Yaconelli and Wayne Rice. Youth Specialities, 1971 ($5.25 each), 861 Sixth Ave., Suite 411, San Diego, CA 92101. Several issues filled with ideas that have worked for people in creative youth ministries all over the country. Crowd breakers, publicity, skits, programming ideas, camp and retreat ideas, and games are included in this resource.

Rap by Lyman Coleman. Serendipity Books (Waco, Texas: Word, Inc., 1972). $3.95. Track One, Relational Labs, pp. 26-34, is suggested for different kinds of activities focusing on *Who Am I?*

Communicating with Junior Highs by Robert L. Browning, rev. ed. How to listen to, learn from, and engage in dialogue with younger teens. (Nashville: Graded Press, 1968). $1.95.

Retreats by Vincent Coletta. From Youth Ministry Administration Kit, Board of Educational Ministries, American Baptist Churches in the U.S.A., 1972. Valley Forge, PA 19481. 25¢. Order from Literature Services, (#LS 13-114) of Judson Book Store, Valley Forge, PA 19481. A small booklet inside a whole packet of goodies which are invaluable for youth ministry wherever! The retreat booklet suggests five kinds of retreats, complete with a schedule of each. Also suggests different settings and objectives for retreats. (Whole packet is $9.95.)

Retreat Handbook by Virgil and Lynn Nelson. (Valley Forge: Judson Press, 1976.) $5.95. Complete handbook for planning retreats with many suggested program ideas.

Respond, Volumes 1, 2, 3, 4
Books of resources for youth ministry. (Valley Forge: Judson Press). $3.95–$5.95 each.

Mrs. Sharon Ballenger is a high school counselor in Omaha, Nebraska, and has worked in youth conferences for several years.

THE MOOLA GAME

What is the value of money?

by WILLIAM M. SHINTO

What is the value of money? This unit of four exercises is devised to explore the meaning of stewardship. Exercise 1, the simulation game, is the heart of the unit. The optimal schedule is four sessions. For a one-session use of the unit, begin with the game (Exercise 2) and then introduce ideas about stewardship in the after-game discussion period.

EXERCISE 1: "One for the Money"

Suggested time: 55 minutes.

Step 1

Ask the group to read Matthew 25:14-30, the parable of the talents. Then discuss the following ideas:

1. *Talents:* The talent, in Jesus' day, was a unit of money worth $1,000. From the use of the word *talent* in the parable comes our use of the word to mean skills, abilities, and intelligence as well as money.

2. *Differences in talents:* Jesus clearly taught that persons have differences in talents (v. 15) but that no one is without some abilities. The equality is not of skills and gifts but of opportunities and responsibility.

3. *Stewards:* The steward is a person entrusted with the property of another. In the parable the various persons were given talents and were expected to use them wisely. There was to be a time of accountability.

4. *Discipline:* The parable teaches that a steward was to exercise a discipline of balance between responsibility and risk. The one-talent person failed, not because he had the least entrusted to him, but because he was fearful. The others took the task with a deeper sense of responsibility and with courage hazarded untried paths.

Step 2

Preparation of the Budget Dollar

Suggested time: 15 minutes.

This step will help the person think through his or her priorities in spending in an ideal situation.

Prepare a chart with a large circle representing a silver dollar and list key categories of expenditures (see figure 1). Each person should also have either a blank sheet of paper or one which has the "dollar" and categories already mimeographed on it.

Explain that the dollar represents an unlimited amount of income and the youth are to decide what percentage they would spend under each category.

The categories are only suggestive, and group participants shoud be encouraged to develop their own categories.

Step 3

After all have worked on their own budgets for a time, have them cluster in triads in order to share and discuss the reasons they chose to divide their "dollar" as they did. The purpose is to share ideas rather than to have others attempt to change the choices.

EXERCISE 2: "Two for the Show"

Suggested time: when only one round is played—60 minutes. Add 30 minutes for each additional round.

Preparation

PERSONNEL:

One director ("God"): is in absolute control. "God" sets rules and all decisions are final.

One person for each "Outlet": Green Avenue Church; House of Sunshine (social services); OJ's Orange Juice Happening (snack shop); The Pink

MY IDEAL BUDGET

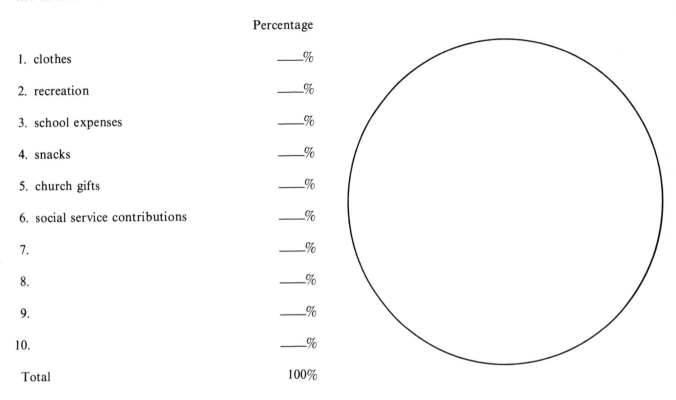

	Percentage
1. clothes	——%
2. recreation	——%
3. school expenses	——%
4. snacks	——%
5. church gifts	——%
6. social service contributions	——%
7.	——%
8.	——%
9.	——%
10.	——%
Total	100%

Figure 1: Worksheet for Computing Ideal Budget

Platter (record shop); Red's Disco-Tek (dance hall); Royal Purple Threads (clothing store). (The number of "outlets" is determined by "God" and depends upon the size of the group. A minimum of three is necessary including either the church or the social services outlet.

One or more police officers: to monitor players.

MATERIALS:

Income slips: (one per player) of varying amounts (i.e., $1, $5, $7, etc.) representing a week's earnings.

Money chits: a supply of plain white slips, each representing a dollar.

Return chits: Each outlet has a supply of return chits—slips of paper in the corresponding color, that is, Green Avenue Church has green chits, etc.

Signs: to identify each outlet.

Badges: for police officers.

Step 1. Instructions

"God" explains the game and the rules. He or she will also act as the timekeeper and may change the rules as the game progresses.

Income: Each player receives an equal amount of allowance (ten white chits). In addition, each player draws an income slip which yields extra money—he/she cashes the slip in: "God" will exchange the slip for "dollars." This gives each player some funds, but all will have varying amounts.

Round of Play: Each round consists of three sections (as explained in step 2 below).

Step 2. Round of Play

1. *Planning* (5 minutes)

   a. Receive cash from income slip and allowance.
   b. Decide whether you are going to play alone or in a team (team limited to three persons).
   c. Decide how you will budget your money for spending at the outlets.
   d. "God" explains what each outlet is and the

return chits one will receive at a particular outlet, that is, church will give five return chits for a dollar; snack shop, three chits; record shop, eight; etc.

(NOTE: "God" *does not* tell players about the exchanging of chits for cash value points. See below under *Counting*.)

2. *Buying* (10 minutes)

   a. You exchange dollars for return chits in outlets where you've decided you will spend your dollars.
   b. "God" has the right to change the exchange rate for any outlet at any time (i.e., if there are too many players trying to buy from one outlet, etc.)
   c. You can make side deals with owners, the church, or a social service worker for a different rate of exchange—*but* you run the risk of being caught by a policeman who can arrest you. You may also have other devious ways of gaining more return chits—also at the risk of being caught. If caught, "God" will mete out a fine for cheating.

3. *Counting* (10 minutes)

   a. God will have a master worksheet (large newsprint or chalkboard) with each player's name and will record the number of chits by color, i.e., Sammy—4 red, 3 yellow, etc.)
   b. "God" will then assign the *cash value* of each color chit. This is a crucial step. "God" will assign *cash values* at a higher rate for the snack shop, record shop, dance hall, and clothing store than for the church or the social service center. Thus, if the church gave five chits per dollar, assign only one cash value point per chit; if the snack shop gave two chits, assign a cash value of ten, yielding twenty points, etc.
   c. Final cash value points will then be totaled for each person. (If a member of a team, each person receives equally from the total of the three.)

Play a second round if time permits. "God" will continue to change the exchange rates for both the return chits and the cash value. The one unvarying rule is that social services and the church contributions always have far smaller cash values and thereby contribute least to the total points.

"God" can decide whether to do the mathematics to determine a winner or just to end the game—remember you are "God"!

Step 3. After Game (20 minutes)

Discussion in groups (suggest that you divide into triads, or if the group is large, into octets.) There will probably be no need for prompting discussions, but if starter questions are needed, here are a few suggestions:

- Was "God" fair? If you were God, how would you act?
- If you acted alone, are you glad?
- If you were on a team, did it work out to your satisfaction?
- After the first round, did you agree with the "cash" value return for exchanging your chits?
- the church contributions and social service outlet did not yield many final points. What other kind of values might have been assigned?
- Was the purpose of the game to accumulate as much cash as you could?
- Was the purpose of the game to win?
- In fact, what was the purpose of the game?
- Are you satisfied that you budgeted right? Did you budget better in the second round? How do you know that you did?
- Were you a good steward of your funds? How do you know that you were?

EXERCISE 3: "Three to Get Ready"

Suggested time: 60 minutes

Step 1

After summarizing what occurred in the first two exercises, give each person two sheets of paper and have him or her mark "needs" at the top of one, and "likes" on the other.

Step 2

Have each one list ten things he/she needs and ten things he/she likes.

Step 3

Have them assign cash values to each item; that is, ten-speed bike, $120; date at school prom, $50; hiking, no cost.

Step 4

When all have finished, have them check off three items from each list of the things they most need and like.

Step 5

Have them divide into triads and discuss their choices and why.

Step 6

Have them regroup as a whole and discuss these questions: What is money? What is a value? How do our values help determine the way we spend our money?

EXERCISE 4: "Four to Go!"

Suggested time: 60 minutes
The final exercise is to do some real life budgeting and planning.

Step 1. Review and Instructions

Have the group discuss the three previous exercises by listing learnings and insights on newsprint or the chalkboard.

Explain that in their lives they have responsibility for managing whatever income they own. Tell them that this exercise is one which can be of practical value.

Step 2. Budget

Ask each person to list all of the income received both from allowance and from earnings from jobs. Have participants look at the first exercise and think through what they need to create a realistic budget. The income in real life is a limitation; the priorities are the key to the budget. Have them keep in mind the relationship between their values and money. Each person should write out a personal budget.

Step 3. Discussion

Discuss in triads if there has been any change in their priorities from exercise 1 to this point.

Step 4. Evaluation and Next Steps

List on newsprint or the chalkboard the positive experiences and negative ones during this unit.

A next step might be to keep a record of actual spending during the next few months and then compare notes again.

William M. Shinto is a national staff member of United Ministries in Higher Education, American Baptist Churches in the U.S.A., living in Costa Mesa, California.

MONEY, MORALITY, AND MYOPIA

A game of moral choices

by PHILLIP H. GILLISPIE

One of the more productive uses for a parlor game is to convert it into a game with a purpose. The following simulation game will illustrate how a junior high youth group (with adult participation) can transform the game *TWISTER* into a game on making moral choices.

The purpose of "Money, Morals, and Myopia" is to stimulate junior highs into thinking concretely about "costs" of moral decisions. Every decision must be placed in a context of self-image, family, friends, and resources. No decision of right and wrong can be made without taking into account the cost in these four areas.

The materials for this game consist of one *TWISTER* game. The game should be supplemented by a sign, placed prominently on the wall, which reads:

> Blue—self-image
> Yellow—relationship to parents
> Red—relationship to peers
> Green—money

Also make a poster which says:

> "Every Decision Has a Price"

Finally, type on three by five cards a series of questions that junior highs would construe as requiring a "moral choice" in order to answer them.

For example:

> "Should I smoke at the weekend slumber party?"
> "Is it enough to just do my history assignment, or should I do it well?"
> "Is it wrong to kiss on the first date?"
> "Should I befriend the girl of another race in my class who was bussed here from across town?"
> "Should I run for youth group president?"

Make up additonal questions that seem appropriate for your group. Write each question individually on a card; mix up the cards; and place them face down on a table near the playing area.

To begin the game, ask one person to operate the "spinner," which for the purposes of this game we will call the "cost counter." Then solicit two volunteers to lead off. One of two initial players stands at each end of the playing cloth. The game will then proceed in the following steps:

1. Each of the two initial players shall draw a card from the pile of "decisions" questions.

2. The card is then read in a loud, clear voice to all persons present.

3. The person operating the "spinner/cost counter" spins and announces the direction (i.e., right foot on red, left hand on green, etc.).

4. Each player follows that direction, and in addition each player, in turn, must tell the group the cost of a positive or negative decision on the question that is posed on the card he or she drew with respect to the appropriate one of the four categories that corresponds to the color indicated on the spinner. For example, a positive choice on smoking might cost lack of self-respect and harm to health, but would gain with peers.

5. The game proceeds with each player going in turn, until one of the players loses his or her balance and falls.

6. When a player falls, he or she must answer the question that was asked on the card.

7. Then a third person draws a card and begins the game and plays in the same manner as the preceding player.

8. Persons continue to replace the individual who falls and must give an answer to the question drawn, until every person has had an opportunity to play.

After each person has had a turn, the participants reconvene as a group and discuss the questions, the cost of decision making, and how different persons responded to the "cost factor."

Phillip H. Gillispie is executive director of the Schenectady Community Action Program, Inc.

SECTION I
Program Resources
About Pop Culture

GROUP STUDY

PROJECTS

TV AND VALUES

Analyzing the values communicated on TV

by WAYNE MAJORS

PURPOSE

To analyze the values communicated on TV programs and to respond to them from a Christian perspective.

> **WHY?**
>
> Television is a major interest of youth today, and its influence on their time and conversation is great. Some youth will identify with the feelings expressed in the poem and share spontaneously (or with a minimum of gentle urging) their experience. If not, the worksheet will help them to develop a new way of looking at television programs.

PREPARATION

The leader may want to choose youth to present the introductory poem and Scripture. If so, they should be chosen in advance and the leader should go over the material with them to clarify its meaning and purpose.

PROCEDURE

Introduction. Present the poem and give a brief introduction to the topic. Ask group members to share experiences similar to those expressed in the poem and to reflect on the meaning of the Scripture in relation to those experiences.

TELEVALUES ???

That TV show gave me a fright!
It ruined my sleep for half the night.
I knew the things they did were wrong;
Yet I enjoyed it all along.
Should I enjoy a show like that?

Where does it say my mind is at?
I watched them steal and kill and fight,
And yet they made it seem alright.
What if my life were lived that way?
An instant rerun every day?
No God, no peace, no love, no hope,
A world that's made of pain and dope?
That's not the world I want to see,
Nor where I want my mind to be.
Next week when that show's on again,
I think I'll turn to channel ten!

—Wayne Majors

Scripture: 1 Thessalonians 5:21-22

> **WHY?**
>
> The values taught by television need to be examined in the light of Christian teaching. The alternative is to allow your mind to absorb blindly the value systems of the programs you watch regularly, without exercising your divine right to *choose* the values you will hold and live out. The worksheet will provide a simple procedure for analyzing programs, evaluating their teachings, and choosing how you will respond.

Presenting the Worksheet

The worksheet can be duplicated for each person in the group, or the leader can read the directions and questions aloud and the group members can write and draw their responses on blank paper. Either way, the leader should do the exercise before the meeting and be prepared to share his or her own responses as an example for each step.

After all have completed their worksheets, gather in a circle, show your drawings, and share your answers.

Try to get at the "why?" behind each response.

Discuss whether your group would agree or disagree with the program's views of what is "good" and "bad," and what God, people, and the world are like.

Close with an act of worship or a prayer related to the experience.

WORKSHEET FOR "TV AND VALUES"

1. Draw a picture in the space below of a TV program you watched recently. Include all of the characters you can remember and put them in a scene from the program.

2. Put a circle around the character you would *most* like to be and put an "X" over the one you would *least* like to be.

3. Complete these sentences:

   a. This program teaches that it is good to _____.

   b. This program teaches that it is bad to _____.

4. Summarize in a few sentences (or a few words) what this program said, in general, about God, people, and the world.

   a. People are _____

   b. God is _____.

   c. The world is _____.

IF YOU HAVE MORE TIME

1. Preparation: Individuals may watch a selected program during the week or the group members may watch it together. Choose a program that offers an interesting story, message, or moral.

2. Reflect on the program by listing together the following:
   a. Numbers you remember seeing or hearing in the program (highway signs, statistics, ages, etc.).
   b. Shapes you can recall (buildings, signs, furniture, scenery, etc.).
   c. Colors you remember.
   d. Sounds you recall hearing.
   e. Quotable quotes you remember. (Did any of the characters say anything that caught your attention?)

3. Analyze the role of music in the program.
   a. How did the music create moods? What moods?
   b. How would the program be different without music?

4. Do the worksheet as a group project and get consensus before writing down responses.
   a. Did the program reflect Christian values?
   b. If so, how? If not, describe the values reflected.

5. Divide the group into small groups and have each invent another ending for the program that will better reflect Christian values. Each group can act out its ending and explain its reasons for ending it that way.

6. Close by standing in a circle and completing this sentence: "One word I would like to say to God about this program is _____."

Wayne Majors is Director of Christian Education at the First Christian Church (Disciples of Christ) in Ada, Oklahoma.

LOOKING OUT FROM THE TUBE

Why some TV programs are popular

by WAYNE MAJORS

PURPOSE

To discover what makes certain TV programs popular and what the popular programs reveal about the values of the audience.

WHY?

Have you ever wondered what it would be like to look out from inside a television picture tube? You would be able to see who was watching and what they were like. In a sense, that's what this program is about. As we look at ourselves, we can discover something about the kinds of persons we are and the kinds of values we have. Our favorite programs may give us a clue about our ideas of good and bad, right and wrong. As we look at ourselves reflected on the TV screen, we may decide to change channels or adjust the picture a little.

We may also gain a clue or two that will help us to understand our world. What kind of values are held by the average person in our society? Look at the TV programs society makes "popular," and those values may be revealed. Once revealed, we may want to celebrate some of them, question some, and reject or change others.

PREPARATION

You will need to gather some crayons and paper, newsprint or a chalkboard, and a large supply of recent issues of a *TV Guide*-type magazine.

PROCEDURE

Introduction. You may wish to share some of the ideas from the "WHY?" section above and introduce briefly the agenda for the program.

Step 1

Hold an election to find the programs that are most popular with your group. Take nominations and list them on newsprint or a chalkboard. Select the top five by consensus, or, if necessary, by majority vote.

Step 2

Divide into groups of three or four, pass out paper and crayons, and ask each small group to draw a picture that shows all of the things the five shows have in common. (All may have a male star; all may be police stories; all may take place in a certain period of history, etc.)

Step 3

Gather and have each small group share its pictures.

Step 4

On newsprint or chalkboard, make a list of all of the things that are in the drawings. This list will give the group an idea of what the audience values. Write across the top of the list "The TV audience values. . . ."

Step 5

Ask the group to make statements about the common elements of the five shows as they reflect the values of the audience. For example: "The audience is more interested in the lives of men than women"; or "The audience enjoys violence and action"; or "The audience prefers the past to the present."

Step 6

Record the statement on newsprint or chalkboard and try to draw out the implications of each.

Step 7

When this list has been completed, remind group participants that they picked the five shows and they are the audience that they have described. Are these statements accurate statements of what they value?

Step 8

Ask: Do these statements reflect Christian values? Compare these values with Romans 12:9-21. How does the collection of TV value statements compare with the values that Jesus taught and exemplified?

Step 9

Close with an act of worship or a prayer that our values might reflect those of Jesus.

IF YOU HAVE MORE TIME

Step 1

Have each person list ten TV shows he/she watches most often.

Step 2

Transfer all of the shows to one group list, being careful not to list the same show twice.

Step 3

By voting or consensus, rank the shows on the group list to pick the ten shows that are the *group's* favorites.

Step 4

Pass out and examine past issues of a *TV Guide*-type magazine to see how the ten shows picked by the group are described. Read the descriptions of several weeks of programs for each show. Discuss any common values or elements that you find and list them on newsprint.

Step 5

As a group, divide the shows into categories, such as police stories, westerns, comedies, news programs, etc.

Step 6

Determine which category contains the largest number of programs and discuss what this says about the values of the audience.

Step 7

As a group, try to describe the audience for each category of shows. What would the people who watch these programs be like? What would their interests probably be? What would be their ideas of "good," "bad," God, people, and life?

Step 8

Remind group members that they are the audience they have just described because they pick the programs. Have they accurately described their own values? Are those values Christian? How do they compare to Romans 12:9-21?

Step 9

Have each person complete the sentence: "The best thing about TV is. . . ." Close with an appropriate act of worship.

Wayne Majors is Director of Christian Education at the First Christian Church (Disciples of Christ) in Ada, Oklahoma.

DEVELOP YOUR OWN MOVIE RATING SYSTEM

Junior highs can grade movies themselves

by EARL JOHNSON

Here are a few ideas for understanding the movie rating system, developing your own, and providing a service.

Step 1

Do research at the public library to determine what the Code and Rating Administration (CARA) of the motion picture industry has decided constitutes restricted viewing for different age groups. You might also be interested in the code the Canadian Film Board uses. Compare the criteria used and the maturity levels defined by the two groups.

STEP 2

Collect film advertisements out of papers and magazines. Make a large poster with four divisions. Each section will be for one of the letter ratings. Compare the ads. What are the different techniques used to "sell" the picture? How are illustrations different? What kinds of adjectives are used to describe films in each category?

Step 3

Write some ads of your own. Take a "G" rated picture and compose an ad as if it were PG, R, or X. Similarly, take an "X" rated film and advertise it as PG, R, and G. How have you sold the picture to a different audience? What adjectives, scenes, or reviewers' words have you used in portraying the film in each category?

Step 4

Make a survey in your community. Interview many different people of various ages and positions. Here are some suggested questions to ask (add your own):

Do you like to go to movies?

What kind of movies do you like?
How do you pick your movies? (ads, friends, reviews)
Do you use the code system in your selection?
Do you think the rating system works?
Is it helpful? Is it fair?
Have you ever disagreed with a rating? What movie?
Do you think we need and should have a rating code?
What do you feel should be restricted viewing? (What wouldn't you want your kids to see?)

Step 5

Go to see a movie as a group. Before you leave, pass out slips of paper giving each person a role (viewpoint from which to watch the movie). Have at least two or three from each of the categories below plus one emcee to run after-show interviews.

advocates	middlepersons	public
producer	theater owner	children (6–10)
director	CARA reviewer	youth (12–16)
editor	reviewer(s)	youth (17–20)
actor(s)		adults (over 21)
		pick a profession:
		minister
		teacher
		doctor
		police
		general
		parents

Step 6

After seeing the movie, the emcee should interview the group. Find out how you felt about the movie as your role-person saw it. You might want to give examples of the following in the movie.

What was: wholesome, sensitive, educational, up-
lifting, relevant, moving, real, intelli-

gent, mature, obscene, cold, unreal, exploitive, stupid, irreverent, violent, fear-producing, bloodthirsty, destructive, enduring, entertaining, enriching? After discussing the film as your role-person saw it, can you discuss it from your own personal perspective? How was it different from your own situation? Be sure you are all back to your normal selves, or your parents won't understand why you came home as Robert Redford.

Step 7

Write your own code. First decide what criteria you will use. Then set up a chart, for example:

age groups:	6–12	13-16	17–20	over 21
criteria				
nudity	no			
sex	no			
violence	limited			
scare	limited			
language	limited			
irreverence	limited			

Now develop your own letter system for each of the categories, for example, GCF for good clean fun or R for raunchy.

Step 8

Make a bulletin board in your church for movie reviews. Post your rating system and explanation, and then keep the review board up-to-date. See movies, discuss them, give your rating, write a review, and then post them on the board for the church community.

Step 9

Keep evaluating your project. How is your system any different from that of the motion picture industry because yours was written for and by a Christian community?

Earl Johnson is a free-lance writer and movie-reviewer living in Connecticut.

FRIDAY NIGHT AT THE MOVIES

Using a movie as program content

by HUBERT HUNTLEY, JR.

A plan for using current movies as junior high program material.

WHY?

Movies provide a three-dimensional view of life while communicating a message. They are "in" with junior highs because at this age imaginations are creative and there seems to be an innate romanticism. One of the real tasks of the junior high leader is to help the individual young person learn to separate fantasy from reality and to help him or her resist the temptation to identify too much with any fantasy story found in film or literature. Filmmakers have "an idea" to put into their work, and this can be a valuable tool for helping junior highs see the reality of life.

PREPARATION

It is important for the leaders (advisors and youth) to check out the film before deciding that it would be a good one for the total group. The current newspaper and magazine reviews and ratings (X= Adults Only, R= Under 17 Admitted Only with an Adult, PG= Parental Guidance Suggested, and G= Family) will be a helpful guide, but the planning team should see the film in order to prepare the group for the total experience. In choosing a film, consider: the price (some older good films are available at $1.00 to $1.50 per seat), the distance to and from the theatre, and the schedule of the youth group itself. Since starting times for the films are varied, be sure to check with the theatre and allow enough travel time so that if you have to wait in line, you will not be late.

One group avoids the high cost of candy at the lobby counter by buying some at the supermarket and then handing it out just as they enter the theatre. This will help save money.

AT THE MOVIE—AND AFTER

The leadership committee should suggest a question or two that the group would look for in the film, such as "What was the main point the producers and directors were trying to get across?" or "What was the hero trying to say by his or her action?" These will provide the basis for discussion after the movie. It should be made clear where you will meet after the movie is over, so that people will not be lost.

While at the movie, the temptation of junior highs sometimes is to have "too good a time" at the expense of the other people in the audience. Loud whispers and excessive movement to and from the lobby can often be distracting; so advisors should seat themselves strategically throughout the group to encourage attention.

Plan to have a time for reflection and discussion at a home or back at the church. It need not be a long time but could give some, who want to, a chance to discuss the feelings and impressions they had. Questions to ask are: What was the theme of the movie? How do you feel about this theme? Do you agree with what the movie said about the theme? With what character(s) did you identify? Why? What did the film say about our Christian faith? Close with a hymn or folk song, Scripture (appropriate and short), and a prayer, all done by the planning committee with the help and support of adult leaders. Refreshments, of course, are always appropriate.

EVALUATION

Be sure to evaluate the program as soon as possible before impressions are lost. One effective way is to evaluate each program on a line graph from 1 to 10, 1 being the worst and 10 being the best. Plan to make suggestions for things you would do again at a similar program or things that you would like to change. Remember, movies tend to exaggerate a theme, making it "bigger than life," and your opportunity is to help translate this into the hopes, dreams, expectations, and faith of the junior high young person.

Rev. Hubert Huntley, Jr., is Minister with Youth of the First Baptist Church of Worcester, Massachusetts.

SECTION I
Program Resources
About Building Community

YEAH, TEAM!

Reflecting on the way we play team sports

by FLOYD E. WELTON

PURPOSE

- To involve junior highs in an intensive sports experience.
- To help them reflect upon their experience.
- To develop some new behavior options.

WHY?

Youth in grades 7 and 8, perhaps 9 also, compete on a number of recreational or school teams. More junior highs are involved in competitive athletics than are senior highs. Although junior highs often are followers and seldom "life-style creators," team sports provide opportunities for testing values and developing patterns for life. Quite often the coach of the school football team, the pony league baseball team, or the softball team unintentionally and unconsciously becomes a model for junior highs.

Even some who don't get involved as players fantasize that they are internationally acclaimed sports heroes with six- or seven-digit salaries and all that goes with celebrity status. So even the spectator is influenced by sports, and values are being reshaped and formed by an illusionary picture.

Starting with some of these silhouettes of reality, this program seeks to involve junior highs in an intensive sports experience, to help them reflect upon their experience and behavior in relationship to values and goals, and then in faith reflection to develop some new behavior options. IMPORTANT: Do not play the game without having the discussion afterward, if you want this to be a learning experience.

PREPARATION

Leaders, preferably an adult and a couple of youth, will facilitate the program by doing the necessary planning and preparation, by explaining the rules of the game, by serving as an official/umpire/timekeeper for the game (perhaps this is the task of the adult leader), by leading the reflection, and by providing direction for worship/closure.

1. Read carefully the rules for the game of Double Goal Soccer which has been created for this program.

2. Select the playing surface. A grassy area near the church building, a large backyard, the church fellowship hall, or the basketball court of a gymnasium are among the possibilities.

3. Secure the ball. An official soccer ball isn't essential. If one isn't readily available, consider a small beachball or a similar light but not too hard ball.

4. Determine the boundaries, establish the goals at each end, and mark the center stripe. Give attention to making the goals sufficiently distinctive to avoid arguments. If possible, discover some way to identify the six-foot height of each of the four goals.

5. Secure a whistle for the umpire. If a stop watch is readily available, secure it for the umpire.

6. Mimeograph or put on newsprint the personal, team, and group debriefing questions.

7. Consider some plans for involving junior highs of the church as participants in the game. It may be necessary to make adjustments to facilitate the participation of youth with special needs or physical limitations.

RULES FOR PLAY

1. The playing field is approximately twice as long as it is wide, but it may be adjusted in size to the number of players. The mouth of each goal is approximately one-fourth of the width of the field with

DOUBLE GOAL SOCCER

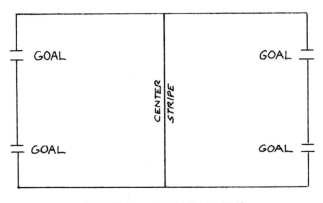

PLAYING FIELD DIAGRAM

a distance of one-fourth of the width between the two goals. For ten players (five per team) a maximum playing surface of 120′ x 60′ is recommended.

2. The minimum number of players required to play the game is six (three per team or two goaltenders and a forward per team.)

3. An inflated ball slightly smaller than a basketball is used. A soccerball is ideal, but a playground ball or a four-square ball may be used.

4. The object of the game is to score a goal at the opponent's end of the field by kicking or butting the ball through one of the goals.

5. As in soccer, a player may strike the ball with any part of the body except arms and hands. If the ball touches the arms or hands of the player, the nearest opposing player is awarded a free kick.

    a. If the infraction occurs on the opponent's side of the field, both goaltenders may defend against the free kick. (On this free kick the goaltenders may not advance more than eight feet from the goal.)

    b. If the infraction occurs on the defensive side of the center stripe, only one goaltender may defend against the free kick. (On this free kick the goaltender may not advance more than fifteen feet from the nearest goal.)

6. The game commences with players of each team taking positions across the field in front of the goals being defended. (Each team lines up on its side of the center stripe.) A player of one team stands between the goals at the end of the field and kicks the ball across the center stripe to the opposing team.

7. A goal is scored when the ball is kicked or butted through a goal not more than six feet off the

ground. After a goal is scored, players return to their team's side of the center stripe and a player of the team scoring the goal kicks off to the opposing team.

8. When the ball goes out-of-bounds, play is halted momentarily and the ball is awarded to the team not touching the ball last at the place where it went out. The ball is put into play with a two-hand overhead throw. When the ball goes out on the defensive side of the center stripe, it must be touched first by a player of the offensive team. When an infraction occurs (the ball is touched by a defensive player before being touched by an offensive player), the ball is returned out-of-bounds to be put in play by the offensive team.

9. The game may be played with any time periods. Four periods of ten minutes each are suggested with teams changing ends of the field after each period. The team scoring the most goals wins the game. In case of a tie, a five-minute sudden death period may be played, with the team scoring the first goal winning the game.

10. After each period, teams exchange ends of the field, defending the opposite goal. If there are irregularities (trees, obstacles, etc.) in the field, the disadvantage to a team may be neutralized.

AFTER THE GAME

Personal Debriefing Questions

Immediately after the conclusion of the game, assemble the youth and distribute the personal debriefing questions or display the questions on newsprint or the chalkboard.

1. On the scale below, check the point which best indicates your *enjoyment of the game.*

1	4	7
low	so-so	high

2. On the scale below, check the point which best reflects your *feelings about the outcome* (final score) of the game.

1	4	7
negative	neutral	positive

Why?

3. On the scale below, check the point which best describes your *style of participation.*

1	4	7
in solo fashion as an individual	?	cooperatively as a team member

4. On the scale below, check the point which best

measures *the amount of energy you expended* in the game.

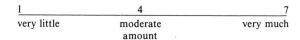

1	4	7
very little	moderate amount	very much

5. On the scale below, check the point which best reflects your sportsmanship (playing by the rules and demonstrating concern for the well-being of other players) during the game.

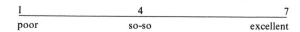

1	4	7
poor	so-so	excellent

Team Debriefing Questions

After the youth have completed the personal debriefing questions, invite the youth to meet as teams in which they competed, with each team forming a group to discuss the three questions. (Take ten to fifteen minutes for these questions.)

1. Invite persons to report out how they checked the various personal questions. Move through the questions one by one.

2. List on newsprint or chalkboard the strengths of your team. (Consider skills, attitudes, and relationships.)

3. List the areas in which improvement is needed. (Again consider skills, attitudes, and relationships.)

Group Debriefing Questions

Bring the two together to form one group. By so doing, the teams are reminded that they are one youth group. Display the questions one at a time and invite youth to respond.

1. If we played Double Goal Soccer again, what might you do differently? (Encourage persons to use the first person singular pronoun.) What might your team do differently?

2. Have the activities of the evening helped any of you to have a better feeling about yourself? Others in the group? The group as a whole? In what ways has this happened?

3. In the playing of the game and the discussion, have you learned or discovered anything about yourself? The group? The positive and negative values of competitive sports? What new insights have you made?

4. In what ways is your life similar to the game played this evening?

Closure Worship

Invite each person to find another person from the opposing team and to sit opposite that person. Provide each group of two persons with a Bible or New Testament, perhaps *Good News for Modern Man*.

1. Ask the older person in the pair to read aloud 2 Timothy 2:5.

2. Invite the younger person in the pair to put the verse into his or her own words and to share that with the partner.

3. Ask the younger person in the pair to read aloud 2 Timothy 4:7 and 8.

4. Invite the older person to put these two verses into her or his own words.

5. With the group, discuss Paul's understanding of competition in relationship to his life.

6. Read Philippians 4:8 to the total group. Give two or three members of the group an opportunity to paraphrase this verse.

7. Form a large circle and conclude with a loud cheer for the group.

8. If appropriate, invite the group to participate in circle prayer, focusing upon the competitive sports in which members of the group are involved and the teams upon which members of the group play.

Floyd E. Welton is Associate Minister of the American Baptist Churches of Oregon with special responsibilities for educational ministries program design and leader development.

POPULARITY AND POLITICS

It takes more than popularity to make a leader

by DAPHNE ANNE GILLISPIE

PURPOSE

This session will raise these questions: What is leadership? What does it do for me? What role do I play in emerging leadership? Am I active or passive? It should help junior high youth realize that being "popular" is not the only criterion for being a leader.

PROCESS

As the group begins to gather, the record player could be on with Simon and Garfunkel's "Sounds of Silence" or "Dangling Conversations" playing. Post on the walls some of the questions given in the "Purpose," and encourage group members to look at them and think about them. When the group has assembled, divide into pairs and ask each pair to reflect on qualities of leadership. Have them think of a specific leader with whom they are familiar and contemplate the following:

Who is the leader?

What is he/she like?

Why do I like-dislike this leader?

These questions should be on a flip chart or chalkboard.

The pairs should take ten minutes to discuss and record answers to the questions. (If the group is restless or seems finished sooner, move on.)

The next step is to move into the large group, preferably a circle, for sharing the findings of the dyads. The sharings should be recorded on a large chalkboard or flip chart. Partners may share each other's findings. Sharing someone else's thoughts is less threatening to the self-conscious junior high. The sharing will vary from fifteen minutes to a half hour, depending on the size of the group.

Now look at the long list of answers for each question, and cross out duplicates. Reflect upon these answers and then have the group think about a recent

school or church election. (The leadership team for this program should already have one in mind.) Consider these aspects of the election:

- process followed to determine leadership
- personalities involved
- criteria used

Discuss each of these openly, pressing for feelings as well as facts about the situation. Try to relate answers to information about leadership where possible. Look for correlations between what they like or dream about (first step) and the reality (election).

SUMMARY

Each person should be asked to meditate upon these questions:

1. Was the leadership in that election determined responsibly?

2. What was MY role in that process? Did I assume any responsibility or accountability?

3. How did I support the process? Did I contribute ideas, time, treasure?

Prayer

(The above questions might be woven into the prayer or some of the responses anticipated.)

O God, we ask for strength and guidance as we seek to know who we are and why we are; give us the courage to participate confidently and not be afraid of rejection.

Amen

Learnings

A strong reinforcement for any session can be found in this final step called "Learnings." Simply list random thoughts, as they come from the participants, on what has been learned as a result of the session. For instance, the group may have learned that popularity need not be the basis for leadership, even in a small youth group. Add these learnings to your scrapbook, yearly log, or a wall of the youth lounge or wherever your group has its PLACE.

Daphne Anne Gillispie is a part-time instructor of English, Schenectady County Community College, full-time mother, and interested worker with youth, Emmanuel Baptist Church, Schenectady, New York.

FEELING LIKE A GROUP

Some ways of expressing community

by BARBARA MIDDLETON

Creating the feeling of being a group, of belonging to something, and of having special friends in a certain place is especially important in communities where teenagers see each other only once or twice a week. Unless some effort is put into developing these ties, the church youth group and often the church itself become lost among the many activities bidding for time and attention in our complex society.

As members of a group become more important to one another, the group's activities and concerns will have a higher priority. In fact there is a "snowball" effect. The more youth enjoy each other, the more they will create opportunities to get together. The more they are together, the closer friends they will become.

WHY?

Such an experience will provide a basis for youth to consider what it means to "love one another," as Christ has commanded, and to explore the nature of the church as a closely knit group of Christians who support each other in their faith and life-style. Junior high youth may not be ready to verbalize these concepts yet, but the foundations for deeper religious experiences and more serious discussions may be laid now.

ENJOYING EACH OTHER

Creating opportunities for teenagers to enjoy being with one another is the easiest form of group-building. Sharing good times and laughter are often the bases for wanting to get together again, particularly if a group is uncomfortable with serious discussion. Don't overlook the value of group games, such as volleyball or dodgeball, and socials for help in this area. Here are some other activities which are fun to do:

1. Sew the Group Together

Have the group sit together in a tight circle. Use a blunt table knife as the needle and tie a long string (nine to ten feet per person) to the end of the knife. "Sew" the members of the group together by letting one person drop the knife down his or her neck or waistband and have it fall out of a pantleg. Then pass the knife to the next person and have him or her do the same thing. There will be lots of laughter as the string is pulled through each member's clothing.

2. Nonverbal Ball Games

This activity is done without speaking, and youth are forced to find other ways to communicate. Let people walk around (maybe to some instrumental music) and greet each other silently. When the music stops, or at some other signal, each member is to "find" a ball (any kind) and pantomime playing with it for a minute. Then let each find a partner and "play ball" with him or her. Sometimes small groups will develop; sometimes an entire group will end up playing volleyball together. Let the youth enjoy their imaginary game for a few minutes; then ask them to end the game and say good-bye to their partner or partners nonverbally. If the members of the group are comfortable talking about feelings they had during the game and as they chose a partner, let them do so now.

3. Cinderella's Slipper

Have everyone in the group remove one shoe and place it in a pile in the center of the room. Then have each person hide his or her other shoe somewhere around the edge of the room. The leader should mix the shoes in the center and, if possible, darken the room.

At a signal, everyone is to rush into the center and

find a shoe. Turn the lights on and let each person discover the owner of the shoe he or she is holding. This is to be done nonverbally and "Cinderella style," by trying the shoe on different persons' feet until it fits.

SHARING OURSELVES

As people share themselves with others, they discover that they can be accepted by those others. They begin to feel that they belong with these others and that they are friends. As the friendships become deeper, people become more willing to share their inner feelings and personal concerns. Here are some easy ways junior high youth can begin to share themselves with one another:

1. Writing Similes

Give each person a pencil and a piece of paper. Ask each to write the first word or phrase which comes to mind when the leader reads the first part of each sentence. Afterward let members of the group share what they have written. Here are sample statements to begin with:

Happiness is ....
Having fun is ....
Freedom is ....
Security is ....
Friendship is ....
Loneliness is ....
Home is ....
Worship is ....
Growing up is ....
Independence is ....

2. Choose a Picture

Cut from magazines a large number of pictures which show people expressing a variety of emotions and in a variety of relationships. Mount these on construction paper or newsprint and post them on the walls around the room. Give the members of the group time to look them all over. Then ask each person to stand beside the picture which means the most to him or her, or which he or she likes best. Let each person share his or her choice, and the reason for it, with the whole group. Don't worry if one picture is chosen more than once, because each person will have his or her own reason for the selection.

GIVING TO ONE ANOTHER

Giving to others is harder and more risky than sharing oneself. One has to feel that he or she has something worthwhile to give and that the gift will be acceptable. But an important part of belonging to a group is the feeling that one can make valuable contributions to the other members and to the group as a whole. Here are some activities which will give members of a group a chance to give of themselves to one another.

1. Gift Giving

Tape a piece of paper to each person's back and give everyone a pencil. Let members of the group go around the room, writing on the back of each person what they feel that person has to give. Stress that comments should be positive.

2. Giving Colors

Have the youth sit in small groups of four or six. Give them a moment for each person to consider the members of his or her small group in silence. Then ask each person to choose a color which symbolizes each member of his or her small group (one color for each person).

Let each person share or "give" the colors he or she has chosen to the people in his or her small group. After everyone has shared the colors, let each person share his or her reasons for those particular choices.

ADDITIONAL ACTIVITIES

There are some activities which also allow the members of a group to share their feelings with one another. However, negative feelings as well as positive may be involved, and care should be taken to see that there is already some trust and acceptance established between the members of the group before these are used.

1. Breaking Into or Out of a Circle

Ask one person to volunteer to be "it." Have the rest of the group form a tight circle. The person who is "it" has to break into or out of the circle. Tell the members of the circle to resist being broken, if possible. The game is over when "it" succeeds in breaking in or out, or when it becomes apparent that "it" cannot break in or out of the circle.

Let "it" talk about how he or she felt during the game. What was it like to be "against" the group? Why did he/she use the methods he/she did? Why did he/she push near certain people, if he/she did?

Other members of the group may also want to share their feelings during the game.

2. Developing a Group Shape

Ask the group members to form a shape, a sculpture using their bodies, that represents the group to them. This is to be done nonverbally; so all plans and ideas must be communicated in other ways. There will probably be lots of chaos at first—and in some groups there will be chaos during the entire activity. Allow the experience to proceed until some shape is formed or until it is apparent that there will not be a shape.

Afterward, let the group members talk about what has happened. Did they experience chaos? How did they feel about that? Did they experience cooperation? How were decisions made and who directed the formation of the shape? In what ways did the shape symbolize the group? What belonging was expressed? Was anyone left out?

3. Tug-of-War

Tell the group members that they are to have a tug-of-war and provide them with a rope. Allow them to work out the game, choosing teams and making rules, and then proceeding with the tug-of-war.

When the game is over, let the group members talk about their feelings during the entire experience. How were the rules made? How were the teams chosen? Did a few people dominate or was the process democratic? Did the group experience cooperation? How did participants experience competition? How did the individual members feel about winning or losing? How seriously did they take something that was "just a game" and why?

Barbara Middleton is a professional church educator who edited Respond, Volume 4.

JUNIOR HIGH FAMILY EXCHANGE

Living with someone else's family can improve living at home!

by JANET DeORNELLAS

PURPOSE

To see what it's like to live in someone else's home.

To look for patterns of communication in family relationships.

To try to identify one's own position in a family by experiencing living with another family.

To provide an opportunity for junior highs to develop techniques in a new situation for better relationships at home.

WHY?

Junior highs often think how lucky their friends are. Now is the opportunity to find out what it's like on the other side of the fence. Promote a study of family relationships by organizing a junior high family exchange.

SOME ALTERNATIVES

Short-term exchange—for a day

Long-term exchange—for several days or a week

Exchange within your own youth group

Exchange intra-city with another church

Exchange long-distance with another city or state

PLANNING FOR THE EXCHANGE

Exchanging within your own group or within the city should not present any financial difficulties.

Exchanges with another city or state could present questions of finance. Transportation from one home to another might be solved if you own a church bus. One group could go by bus to the church in the visiting city, and then the bus could return home with the exchange junior highs. The two churches could split the transportation expense. Otherwise, a car pool from City A might deliver the junior highs while City B might be responsible for returning them. Junior highs might pay any recreational expenses from their own funds, but the exchange family would provide all meals, etc.

In setting up an exchange, some families may need to exchange a girl for a girl or boy for a boy because of bedroom facilities. Families should specify if they would prefer a boy or a girl.

Contact a youth group with whom you would like to work out an exchange. First determine the time period, the transportation, and other procedures you have agreed on so that you can give the exchange group clear-cut information about the project.

EXCHANGING FAMILIES

Contract

Live with your exchange family for the time specified. Share in their lives, their activities, and their discussions.

Observe differences and similarities between your families.

Notice

How are problems solved?

Is each member of the family important?

What are the positive experiences of their family life?

Plan an opportunity to discuss topics.

Topics for Discussion with Exchange Family

Church Youth Group: What activities do they have?
Who plans them?
What exciting programs have they had?

Do youth serve on boards in their church?

Family: What do they do together?

What vacations do they take?

What work responsibility do junior highs have?

How much allowance do they receive?

Does the family have "council" meetings to discuss problems and make decisions?

How supportive are family members of one another?

Does the family have many relatives in their community?

BACK HOME EVALUATION

With Family: What have you learned about your own family relationships?

How can they be improved?

What would your parents like to change?

What would you like to change?

What promotes family communication?

Would a family council or sharing time be helpful?

With Youth Group: What have you learned about yourself?

What have you learned about your family?

How was the family exchange most helpful to you?

Janet DeOrnellas was a Director of Christian Education in Jacksonville, Illinois. She is a school teacher, advisor to the youth board of the Great Rivers Region of American Baptist Churches, and a junior high camp director.

IS POLITICS A DIRTY GAME OF MANIPULATION?

Church people need to be involved in community politics

by DAPHNE ANNE GILLISPIE

This project will help to dispel two myths: (1) involvement in politics is dirty; (2) church people ought not to mess in politics. In coming to grips with each of those myths, you will be speaking directly to the following goals of this project: to become familiar with the political process of your town, city, or county; and to learn that political involvement *requires* our participation because that is where significant decisions are made which directly affect our lives. If the Christian church washes its hands of political involvement, we may well pave the way for many more Watergates.

The following plan will need to be tailored to the needs and political structure of your own locale. For example, if you are in a small town with only a town clerk, your project will be less elaborate and time-consuming than that of a large city. The time for the project will necessarily differ as well. Your leadership team should decide a reasonable timetable which may be more or less than the two to three weeks suggested here.

I. LOCAL POLITICS: HOW IT WORKS

The project needs to be introduced as a three-week *adventure* in discovering how decisions are made in your locale. After introducing the project as an adventure, raise questions about why the group might think that this is an important avenue to explore. Keep these answers to be used in session 3.

Assignment 1: Locate the party in power. This may already be known, but urge group members to research it on their own. Also list all elected officials in the MINORITY and MAJORITY parties. (Find this out at the county courthouse, public library, or mayor's office.)

II. LOCAL POLITICIANS

At the second session, share and discuss the results of the first assignment. Talk about the functions of officials, such as the county chairperson, committee men/women, ward chairpersons, etc.

Assignment 2: Seek out one of the officials to talk to and discuss specifically his/her role in a recent decision made in your community. Find out how the official voted and why.

Report at the next meeting the findings of each researcher. Some may have found the committee person very open and accommodating; others may have had no real response. Try to encourage the youth to discover why this might be so. Elected officials have a responsibility to be accountable to their constituency, speaking openly about their voting. Sometimes this information is hard to get.

III. HOW DECISIONS ARE MADE

In this final session it might be helpful to role-play a city council meeting or a town meeting where a decision is going to be reached concerning the erection and funding of a teen center. Using some of the information just gathered, cast the roles that most likely resemble your political structure. Is a decision reached? What are the forces for and against the teen center? Why are political decisions hard to make?

Before concluding this session, look again at the answers from session 1 on why this political avenue is important to explore. Do any of these answers seem more pertinent now? Less? Why? Add to this list of early answers a new list of LEARNINGS. What specifically have I learned from this adventure?

Suggest that the youth who show real enthusiasm find a way to canvass for a candidate or in some manner work for a local candidate for public office. Also, if there are persons in your church who are actively involved in politics, they might either speak to the group or help the group interpret some of its data.

Use as many resources from your local congregation as you can.

CONCLUSION

Democracy is based upon an educated citizenry. If we are to become a part of that educated citizenry, we really need to know how decisions are made and become a part of that process.

Prayer: Dear Father, guide us in our growing and help us to know what is ethical, just, and compassionate. We know that our destinies are intertwined with those of our brothers and sisters and that decisions should not be made in a vacuum. In the name of Christian love. Amen.

Daphne Anne Gillispie is a part-time instructor of English at Schenectady County Community College and a lay worker at Emmanuel Baptist Church, Schenectady, New York.

FLEXING OUR MUSCLE WITHIN THE BODY LIFE

A weekend retreat for an intergenerational group

by W. BERKELEY ORMOND

PURPOSE

To create a climate in which youth and adults can experience some things they have in common and realize that they are an integral part of one another's lives within the community of believers.

> **A GIVEN**
>
> This retreat is designed with the local church in mind, and it is assumed that those participating have a knowledge of the church, its life-style, and its programs.

PLACE

This retreat can be held at a church camp, a local church building with a social or assembly hall, or in a public camping area where there are areas set aside for "group" use.

TIME

This retreat is designed for Friday evening, all day Saturday, and Sunday through noon.

✓ YOUR GET-READY LIST

( ) Select the retreat location.
( ) Firm up the dates.
( ) Set the fees.
( ) Name transportation chairperson/committee.
( ) Name food/menu chairpersons/committee.
( ) Name recreation chairperson/committee.
( ) Name program facilitators/committees:
    ( ) Friday evening
    ( ) Saturday morning
    ( ) Saturday evening
    ( ) Sunday morning

( ) Publicity:
    ( ) Invitations to youth AND adults (Remember: this is an intergenerational experience; so include ample numbers from both generations).
    ( ) Where event will be held.
    ( ) When the event will be held: all hours that have been scheduled should be shared well in advance. This gives your retreat great credibility—something well planned in advance and worthwhile.
    ( ) All costs.
    ( ) What to bring: include ALL articles.
( ) Preparations in advance:
    ( ) Snack-time goodies: We will be spending two evenings together. Bring some type of snack food to be shared at the conclusion of each of the evening experiences.
    ( ) Celebrate yourself with a banner: On Friday evening you will be invited to introduce yourself with a personal banner. On some type of background material, measuring 24 inches by 24 inches, create (at home) a banner which will include:
        your name,
        your school or occupation,
        your favorite "something" (hobby, food, sports, etc.).

AND NOW THE MOMENT OF REALITY OF IT ALL

Friday P.M.

4:00 P.M.—Registration and housing assignments
6:00 P.M.—Buffet supper or "bring your own sack

95

lunch" supper; provide beverage. This type of meal allows for different arrival times.

7:30 P.M.—WAVE YOUR BANNERS HIGH!
Each person will be invited to share his/her life and banner. Use masking tape or thumb tacks to affix these to the walls (or trees if you are at a camp). If possible, let them remain up all during the retreat.

9:00 P.M.—Devotions: Base a 15-minute meditation upon the "body life" concept in Ephesians 4. This will set the theme for the entire retreat.

9:15 P.M.—Snack time

Saturday A.M.

8:00 A.M.—Breakfast: work out morning devotionals with your program chairperson/committee.

9:30 A.M.—GIFT GIVING NEVER STOPS
Objective: To become aware of the variety of gifts (talents) within the body life called the local church and to share and encourage the discovery of gifts within persons.
You will need:
   construction paper
   masking tape
   felt-tip markers or crayons
   pipe cleaners

Fantasy: Divide into several groups so that there are about eight or ten persons in each group. Work toward balance between youth and adults. Keep it intergenerational. Share: "If I could be given a gift, I would like it to be _____ because _____. Continue until everyone who wishes has shared. Feel free to discuss contributions which are not clear. Reassemble.

Facilitator reads Romans 12:1-8 with particular attention to the various gifts or abilities within the body life. Develop some thoughts along that line to serve as a springboard for the next phase. Allow no longer than ten minutes.

INTERGENERATIONAL CREATIVITY

Number off in small intergenerational groups of about five or six. Give each group some construction paper, masking tape strips, and a felt-tip marker. Invite group participants to build a three-dimensional replica of their church. Pieces can be "glued" together by using the masking tape. As the church building is being put together, name each part with one of the "gifts" you see

evident in the church. Example: one person may want to write CELEBRATION on one of the outside walls. Use the felt-tip marker to write these words. Make the project a group-process experience. Allow each person freedom to interpret the gifts; something is a gift if one feels that it is. Talk and share feelings as the church is being built. Allow approximately thirty minutes for this phase.

INDIVIDUAL GIFT SHARING

Pass out a pipe cleaner to each person. Allow about ten minutes for the individual to reflect upon the gift he or she has to contribute to the church. Invite the person to fashion a symbol of that gift with the pipe cleaner, such as a music note if the gift is some form of music. After ten minutes, invite individuals to share their gifts and comments as they place the symbols inside the church. Affirm each other as the gifts are shared.

CLOSING

Have each group bring its church to the assembly area and place it around a candle on a stand. Let the candle represent the Holy Spirit, the energizer and sustainer of gift discovery and growth. Light the candle. Form a circle around all the churches and sing/pray "Spirit of the Living God."

Saturday P.M.

12:00 noon—Lunch

1:00 P.M—Recreation: See the Recreation Section in this book for suggestions, or plan some informal sports in which both generations can participate, such as Frisbee, volleyball, hiking.

5:30 P.M.—Supper

7:30 P.M.—RIBBONS AND BOWS OR KNOTS AND SNARLS
Objective: To help discover those ties that bind generations together within the church and to check out some feelings about these ties.
You will need:
   small ball of string for each group,
   a pair of scissors for each group.

Facilitator reads 1 Corinthians 12, selecting verses from the chapter which will substantiate the unity concept. Secure from an encyclopedia a diagram or body chart which shows the synoptic muscle and nerve system. Stress how the body is "tied" together. Allow a ten-minute time period for this.

INTERGENERATIONAL TUG AND PULL— HANG ON AND RELEASE

Divide into intergenerational groups of six or eight persons. Each person ties a piece of string around his/her waist. From this point on, each person ties another piece of string from his/her waist to the waist string of persons in the group, explaining this "tie" each time it is made. Example: an adult may have a "tie" to each of the youth because he/she was named a youth advisor by the church. One young person may be tied to another young person because they both play on the same team at school. Keep this up until all who wish to do so have tied themselves to others in the group.

All during the process individuals may pull on the ties to indicate a reluctance to have that tie ever broken, or a person should feel the freedom to pick up the scissors and cut any tie he or she feels is too controlling or uncomfortable. This should be done with explanations. Never leave persons in a quandary about your reactions. In both events, pulling the ties tightly and cutting them, the group should be alert and aware of what is happening. Discuss freely, openly, and with honesty. Keep the body life going—the blood flowing by reacting. When ties are cut, make some supportive and affirming gestures to tie it back together.

CLOSING

Reassemble in a large group. Form a circle and share "The strongest tie in my life is _____ between me and _____." After each person has shared in this way, invite a unison response like this: "Thank God for (mention the tie the person just shared.)"

When all who wish to do so have shared, close with this prayer or one of your choice:
Show us, good God,
  the ties we must keep,
  the ties we must break,
  the ties we must seek,
  the ties we must forgo
  if we are to serve thee more effectively
  within the body life
      called *(give the actual name of the church or organization sponsoring the retreat).*
                                                    Amen.

Snack time.

Sunday A.M.

8:00 A.M.—Breakfast
9:30 A.M.—PUTTING IT ALL TOGETHER ON A MOMENT'S NOTICE
  Objective: Provides an opportunity to experience an intergenerational Bible study and a worship/celebration event growing out of spontaneity and creativity.
  You will need:
    large mailing envelopes
    construction paper
    paste
    ribbons
    plastic flowers
    pieces of cloth
    feathers
    any other materials to be used in creative art
    the Lord's Prayer "sectioned off" on as many 3″ x 5″ cards or slips of paper as there will be small groups.
  Important: Divide all the materials above and place in a large mailing envelope along with a "section" of the Lord's Prayer in each. Also paperclip a piece of newsprint to each envelope. Pile in the center of the assembly area or in front.
Facilitator leads in a brief worship experience using the Lord's Prayer as the Scripture. Divide into small intergenerational groups of four or five. (Packets will have been made up in advance and should be assembled at the front.) Each group sends a person to the pile of packets and simply selects a packet for his or her group.

Spend approximately thirty minutes discussing the section of the Lord's Prayer in the packet, and on the piece of newsprint create a banner out of the packet materials based on the section of the Lord's Prayer in the packet. Decide upon a three-minute worship/celebration input when the large group reassembles. Be creative in your worship/celebration moments.

Reassemble.

In sequence (as the Lord's Prayer appears in the Bible), have each group present its banner and worship/celebration input. The facilitator may want to use masking tape to put these banners together to create a mural effect.

CLOSING

The facilitator invites the group to repeat phrases of

the modern translation of the Lord's Prayer, below.
Group may be standing in "friendship circle" fashion
(*arms crossed and hand of next person grasped*).

Father in heaven, *(repeat)*
May everything praise you. *(repeat)*
Rule as you wish. *(repeat)*
Achieve what you want on earth—as in heaven.
(repeat)
Give us each day what we need; *(repeat)*
And forgive us the wrong we have done, *(repeat)*
As we forgive those who have wronged us. *(repeat)*
And guide us away from temptation: *(repeat)*
Release us from evil *(repeat)*
for you are our mighty and glorious king *(repeat)*
And always will be. *(repeat)*
Amen. *(repeat)*[1]

12:00 noon—Lunch
          Departure

Rev. W. Berkeley Ormond is pastor of the Cedar Hills Baptist Church, Portland, Oregon.

[1] Caryl Micklem, ed., *Contemporary Prayers for Public Worship* (Grand Rapids: Wm. B. Eerdmans Publishing Co., 1967). Used by permission.

ESCAPE TO REALITY!

A retreat for junior highs and their families

by JANET DeORNELLAS

To help junior highs build better relationships with their families. (All family members or as many as possible should attend the retreat.)

INTRODUCTION

A retreat provides an opportunity for working on relationships over a longer period of time than the usual one- to two-hour sessions. As the word "retreat" implies, it is a break from the usual routine of life. The retreat theme "Escape to Reality" implies genuineness with meaningful relationships of open, honest communication.

Total commitment by the participants to the period of time set aside for the retreat is necessary for its success. Most retreats profit from a set of guidelines or rules for the occasion. These should be kept to a minimum and should encourage total participation in the experiences and should encourage harmony and caring from the members. For example, "EVERYBODY DOES IT!" includes sharing in planning, participating in all activities, cleaning up, etc. Relationships are strengthened by shared experiences which are rewarding, challenging, and enjoyable.

PREPARATION

Set up a planning committee of several junior highs, a couple of parents, and youth advisors. Establish a date or dates with a tentative time schedule for activities. Secure a location. Some alternatives are:

1. Overnight at the church (Friday 7 P.M. to Saturday 8 A.M.).
2. Sunday at the church (1 P.M. to 9 P.M.).
3. Overnight at a camp setting (7 P.M. Friday to 7 P.M. Saturday or Friday evening to Sunday afternoon).
4. One day at a camp setting or a park (10 A.M. Saturday to 8 P.M. Saturday).

Depending on the location and length of the retreat, plans will need to be made for meals and bedding. At a camp, usually cots are available and only sleeping bags or sheets and blankets are needed. If you camp out, tents also need to be secured.

Organizing committees for areas of responsibility is one way to see that everyone gets involved and also helps accomplish the purpose of the retreat. See that each committee is composed of an adult and a youth co-chairperson plus several youth and adults, depending on the size of your group. In small groups, the responsibility might be assigned to one adult and one youth.

SUGGESTED COMMITTEES AND RESPONSIBILITIES

Invitations: It is very important to include as many junior highs and their families as possible. Personal phone calls or visits are advisable.

Food: Decide how many meals are involved in the retreat and whether or not you plan to do the cooking. Simple meals are preferable so that participants do not spend too much time in food preparation. If all share in this chore, the building of relationships can take place here also. If you need only one meal and stay at the church, an order-in meal, such as a box lunch of fried chicken, is a simple procedure. Breakfast simply might be juice, rolls, and milk or coffee.

Transportation: This committee is necessary if you plan to travel away from the church and need to recruit cars or a bus. Be sure adequate space is available if tents, sleeping bags, and food must be transported.

Music: Select the music before the retreat and include a variety of fun songs plus hymns and folk songs. It would be helpful to mimeograph song sheets because many folk songs are unfamiliar to adults. Music should be an integral part of the retreat. Informal songs may be used around the campfire or used spontaneously around the tables after meals. If you have a member who plays guitar, use it. A variety songbook is *The Good Times Songbook* by James Leisy (Nashville: Abingdon Press, 1974).

Recreation: Plan according to the location of the retreat and length of time. If swimming or canoeing is planned, provision should be made for equipment and safety. Indoor games might include Ping-Pong, relays, sponge ball or invisible ball (pass, kick, toss, throw a make-believe ball). Out-door games might include Frisbee, Wiffle ball, volleyball, or hikes. In selecting recreation, remember the age span that will be represented in your retreat. For example, Wiffle ball or Frisbee do not depend on size or strength to be able to play.

Program: Plan the total schedule and coordinate all other committees and activities. This committee should establish the cost per person or determine otherwise how expenses will be covered. Each retreat program should provide for a variety of fellowship, study, and worship. Depending on the length of the retreat, activities should be selected according to the group, facilities, and suitability. The program committee should select activities, but responsibility for directing them can be assumed by various youth and adult leaders. REMEMBER, junior highs prefer "doing" to "discussion."

SAMPLE SCHEDULE FOR AN OVERNIGHT RETREAT AT A CAMP SETTING

Friday

6:00 P.M. Arrive and move into cabins.
7:00 P.M. Introductions. Sitting in a large circle, say: "My name is. . . . One important thing about me is. . . ."
7:30 P.M. Discussion Starter on Relationships. Fill out individually. Then discuss in groups of three or four.
8:00 P.M. Recreation: Wiffle ball.
9:00 P.M. Snacks and music around the campfire.
? Lights out (agree on time beforehand).

Saturday

8:00 A.M. Breakfast
9:00 A.M. Active Bible study
10:00 A.M. Fingerpaint feelings
11:00 A.M. Fishbowl
12:00 A.M. Lunch
1:00 P.M. Recreation: swimming, boating, hiking, relaxing
3:30 P.M. Role play
4:00 P.M. Worship
4:30 P.M. Evaluation
5:00 P.M. Dinner
6:00 P.M. Go home!

RESOURCES FOR RETREAT

Discussion Starter on Relationships (copy needed for each participant)

Each person completes one.   X for true   O for false

—— 1. If you love someone, you don't get angry with him or her.
—— 2. Love should be reserved for a few persons.
—— 3. You can care about a person without loving him or her.
—— 4. Love is only for married people.
—— 5. Sex should not be discussed in church groups.
—— 6. Discipline is a measure of love.
—— 7. My feelings are an important part of me.
—— 8. The older a person is, the wiser this person is.
—— 9. Each individual has a right to privacy.
——10. Each member of a family should help in making family decisions.
——11. There are few persons with whom I share my innermost feelings.
——12. My family discusses problems openly and shares ways to solve them.
——13. The church is an important part of our family.
——14. I know that many people love me.
——15. "Love your neighbor" is easier than "love your family."

Active Bible Study

Love: 1 Corinthians 13:1-13 and Matthew 22:34-40.
Forgiveness: Matthew 18:21-22 and 6:14-15; Luke 17:3-4.
Prodigal Son: Luke 15:11-32.
Recycling: Ecclesiastes 1:1-11.
Time: Ecclesiastes 3:1-8.
Active Bible study is just what the word "active" implies. Do it instead of discussing it.

1. Try rewriting the passages by assigning one passage to a group of three to five, depending on group size. Instruct the groups to rewrite the main content of the passage in their own words. The original group revision is shared with the total group.

2. Suggest that the groups act out the message of their Scripture for the other groups. Allow about thirty minutes for preparation.

3. Have each group make suggestions of specific ideas for living out the message of the Scripture.

   a. What can I do differently in my life?

   b. How will our family change if we practice these truths?

   c. What changes need to be made in our church?

Select one of these methods or try a variety of them, depending on the length of time.

Fingerpaint Feelings

WHY?

Some media are equalizers. That is, they put adults and youth on similar levels or at least place youth in an area where they may feel as capable as adults. Fingerpainting tends to bring out the "child" in both adults and youth. Fingerpainting is a freeing activity that encourages individual expression.

SUPPLIES NEEDED

White shelf paper in 18″ x 24″ sections

Liquid starch (easy to dispense from plastic catsup or mustard bottles)

Dry tempera paint

Old newspapers

Washbasin and water for washing

Old shirts to cover any good clothes

GUIDELINES

Suggest that each person paint two pictures— one showing feelings of ALONE and one for feelings of TOGETHER. Then put these aside to dry, but if possible where they can be viewed by others. Set up a table where a maximum of six or eight can fingerpaint at one time. Make certain that both adults and youth are at the table at the same time. As they finish, others take their places. Those who are finished should discuss in groups of two or three what they like doing alone and what they like doing with others. Some of these pictures might be shared or displayed for the worship.

Fishbowl

WHY?

This method allows one group to discuss and yet allows the total group to participate by listening.

Inside Group Discusses
Outside Group Listens

Have the adults sit in a circle inside a circle of youth. For about five minutes, the adults discuss, "What bugs me about kids." During the discussion, the youth listen. Then the youth share what they heard the adults say. The youth then get in the inside circle and discuss, "What bugs me about adults." Follow a similar procedure for topics of "What I love about kids" and "What I love about adults."

Role Play

WHY?

Make believe you are someone else. Role play helps you see how someone else thinks and feels. Problems can often be solved when we understand one another.

When assigning roles, select individuals who will not freeze up but who also will not overdo and fall out of character. Give individuals a different role than they have in real life. Observers should be instructed beforehand to watch and determine if the discussion is genuine. What are the problems of communication?

The role play should be stopped after about five minutes. Then allow the actors to share their feelings. After about five minutes' discussion from the actors, open the discussion to the total group. How well did participants stay in their roles? Was a decision reached? If so, how? Did family members really listen to the other members?

Role-play topic: Decide where to go on a family vacation.

Characters:

MR. JACKSON: He would like to go to a lake, stay in a cabin for a week, and go fishing.

MRS. JACKSON: She would like to go to the city, stay in a motel, and eat all meals out so she won't have to cook. She likes to shop in nice stores.

JOY JACKSON *(Age 14):* She wants to go where

there are other teenagers. She doesn't want to leave her friends.

JEFF JACKSON *(Age 12):* He likes to swim and waterski. He plays on a softball team and doesn't want to miss any ball games.

JASON JACKSON *(Age 8)*: He likes to fish and wear grubby clothes.

Worship Suggestions

Worship is most meaningful when it grows out of shared experiences. It should be a shared responsibility of the total group. When, and the number of times you worship, will depend upon the needs of the group. Certainly it should try to capture the joy of new and deeper relationships.

1. A yell might be incorporated to celebrate FAMILY. Spontaneous sharing, such as "It was fun to fingerpaint," with a group response of "Thank God for families!" following each individual's statement is a good way to affirm positive experiences.

2. Scripture selections might be those already studied or others of your choice, such as Psalm 100. Choral reading of Scripture is an opportunity to involve more persons, and it adds variety to the worship experience.

3. Prayer might be a volunteer circle prayer, "I thank God for. . . ."

4. Music should be selected by the music leaders from those songs that have become meaningful to the group during the retreat.

Evaluation

Evaluation should be brief but should pull the learnings from the retreat. It can be a verbal sharing or can be written for later reflection. For example: How has this retreat changed our relationships? What has been positive about this retreat? Other comments.

RESOURCE BOOKS ABOUT RELATIONSHIPS

Sneetches and Other Stories by Dr. Seuss (New York: Random House, Inc., 1961).

The Giving Tree by Shel Silverstein (New York: Harper & Row, Publishers, 1964).

Janet DeOrnellas was a Director of Christian Education in Jacksonville, Illinois. She is a school teacher, advisor of the youth board of the Great Rivers Region of American Baptist Churches, and a junior high camp director.

YOUR OWN SIMULATION GAME ON PARENTS

Creating your own game and understanding parents while doing it

by PHILLIP H. GILLISPIE

Many persons are reluctant to design a simulation game because they have a lack of confidence in their own ability. My only word of caution to the beginning game designer is: Do not be too cautious!

The first step in designing a game is knowing what a simulation game is. I still rely on a definition I developed for my book, *Learning Through Simulation Games.*

> The simulation game, a unique learning tool, has two basic parts. As a simulation it contains a structure, an artificial environment, and a representation of reality. The structure may be as rigid and complex as the moon-landing simulator used by astronauts to prepare for their "real landing on the moon" or as simple as a table placed in the middle of the room representing a school cafeteria. The second irreducible part of a simulation game is role-playing, in which the participants represent an idea, a group, or defined persons. This gaming aspect of the simulation game adds the dynamic to the simulated setting, and they jointly create the context for this unique learning experience.[1]

Using this definition as a background, a game designer needs only to formulate and follow an outline for writing a game. The outline that has proved most effective for me is:

1. Choose an objective.
2. Identify the major systems that relate directly to the issue that is stated in the objective.
3. Specify one problem to solve that typifies the issue identified in the objective.
4. Impose a structure on the game.

Once the game designer has determined what he/she would like to accomplish, the task of building a structure to house the game becomes a relatively easy matter. For the purposes of this article we are considering the writing of a game on the relationships between junior highs and their parents. Think about designing a game around the primary places that youth and parents interact: the kitchen table, a youth

[1]Phillip H. Gillispie, *Learning Through Simulation Games* (Paramus, N.J.: Paulist-Newman Press,) p. 226.

group meeting, an encounter at school, or some other common point of dialogue. The designer could choose a problem that is common to most youth and parents and construct a way of solving the problem in different settings. Having youth play the role of a parent and vice versa is an effective way of helping the two groups understand one another's feelings and reactions.

Another tactic might be to take a simple game like Tic, Tac, Toe and adapt it to your purposes (i.e., building a better relationship between youth and adults). Ask two persons (a youth and a parent) to play three games of Tic, Tac, Toe simultaneously, with each game being labeled as a different aspect of the relationship. The game may go something like this:

RELATING

The purpose of the game *Relating* is to develop a significant relationship with another person while playing the game Tic, Tac, Toe. The playing board is a simple set of three Tic, Tac, Toe sets, labeled as follows:

PEER GROUP　　　THE RELATIONSHIP　　　FAMILY

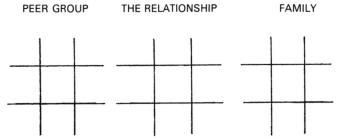

The object of the game is *not* to score a tic, tac, toe in any of the three sets. In other words, if one player "wins," both lose; and if neither wins, both win. The players must cooperate to see that neither player finds it possible to score a tic, tac, toe.

The game is played by a parent and a youth (each may play his/her own roles, or they may switch and one can play his/her own parent or with the parent of a friend) and could proceed as follows:

1. One player chooses X and the other O.

2. The player with an X begins by marking one of the sets on the right or the left.

3. When the X is placed, that person must make an honest statement about him/herself as it relates to the peer group or family (if the player is playing the role of someone else, he/she makes an honest statement about what he/she believes to be true with the person whose role he/she is playing). Examples: "Our family always has family night on Friday." "The neighbors consider me open-minded on child-rearing."

4. Next O follows suit: He/she places an O in one of the two outer sets and reveals a statement about him/herself.

5. After each player has placed at least two marks in the outer two sets, he/she may (*not* must) place a mark in the center set.

6. When a mark is placed in the center set by one player, the other player may ask the player who has placed the mark any question he/she desires. (It is possible for the players to agree in advance that certain types of questions are out-of-bounds.) The player who is asked the question must respond honestly.

7. The game proceeds with the players taking turns by making at least two marks in the outer sets between marks in the center set; revealing a "truth" statement when marking in the outer sets, and responding to a question when marking in the center set; and attempting to reach a stalemate in all three sets.

BONUS

It is possible to achieve a bonus by marking a set in a way that either player could "win" if a mark were placed in the identical box. For example:

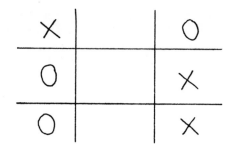

In this case both players may agree to play simultaneously and place ⊗ in the middle box. When this occurs, each player may ask the other a question relating to the set the action occurs in. In the event it occurs in the center set, each player may ask the other player two questions.

There are many ways to alter, add to, or adapt this game. The designer can construe various bonuses or penalties for different configurations. The important thing is to let the imagination run. The sets can be given different labels and the way of approaching the game can be changed.

As you seek to use, write, or alter simulation games, allow them to pull creativity from you and from the participants. Also remember that the game is not the end; it is merely a technique to achieve a learning goal.

Phillip H. Gillispie is Executive Director of the Schenectady Community Action Program, Inc.

SECTION II
Worship Resources

WORSHIP BEGINS IN LIFE

Sensing God and Saying "Yes"
Worship notions and resources

by RICHARD D. ORR

Where does a feeling of worship start in a person? What generates a sense of awe or deepness or "thank-you" or "I'm sorry" or "yes!" to life? What invites a person to sense order and goodness at the "heart" of things? What calls us to look inside and sense mystery and potential for "more"? What suggests a commitment to a loving/forgiving life-style?

These are questions to live around. Both adult leaders and junior highs can use them as guidelines in their attempts to discover the emerging meanings of living. The Christian pilgrimage is a "walking" with questions like these. Such questions help us generate our own particular, and changing, set of answers and directions.

Because the questions are large and the answers still incomplete, the invitation to worship is an invitation to celebrate change. To grow is to change. Our society is changing. Change is so apparent we might say it is a "constant" to count on.

Junior high persons are in a life-spot during which change and growing are major work. Creation and the Creator God are evident in this change. We worship the God who gives order in this process of change. The miracles of these "growings" are awesome mysteries and astounding discoveries. We say "yes" to them from our commitment to God who creates the order in which growing and choices for growth are possible.

Worship does not take place in an isolated vacuum, removed from the changes of life and society. Worship emerges from seeing "miracles" in the everyday. Reverence grows from being surprised by joy or love or even sadness. Worship bursts out of our living experiences as response to mystery, to questions, and to goodness discovered. We are touched by life, and we need a place to say, "Yes!"

All these "high-sounding" words of description are meant to put worship in its "place." For junior high persons, worship is not necessarily in a "spot" removed from life, but in a direct conversation with their daily experiences. A checklist for preparing worship experiences might include:

Is the language of the "celebration" the language of youth?

Are the problems, questions, and joys to which we are addressing ourselves drawn from the real lives of these real persons with whom we work?

Do the place and postures (circles, rows, floors, rooms) fit youth and their comfort? Comfort is not so much physical as emotional. Is this a spot and an act in which youth would "feel okay" expressing themselves?

PLANNING FOR WORSHIP

Worship can be simple or complex, having many steps or one. Preparing opportunities for worship can be a creative act of fitting life experiences with words and expressions. Creativity may need some stable "hooks" on which to hang opportunities for expressing. The following outline is submitted as one set of "hooks" (you can invent your own!). This is an order within which to plan opportunities to say "yes" to God and one's life.

The steps are defined in column one. Columns two, three, and four are faith, need, and Bible thoughts that show the ideas behind such an order. They are not necessarily words and passages to be used in the worship. They merely give the reasons for suggesting these steps.

THREE OPINIONS
"COMMERCIALS" ABOUT WORSHIP

1. We Need to Invent Rituals

Somehow we in the American church have developed a suspicion of anything labeled "ritual." Perhaps we thought a ritual was, by definition, empty of meaning. As a result, much of our worship does not

STEPS IN AN ORDER OF WORSHIP	FAITH IDEAS	HUMAN NEEDS
GATHERING: Any act to invite the community of faith to express its belief and life.	—Christians as "community" —Our call to be a worshiping people —Order out of chaos —Pilgrims on a quest together	—Inclusion/belonging —Our need for significant others —The need to look beyond self for resources —The need for invitation, permission to express
HEARING THE WORD: Opening oneself to the messages of Judeo-Christian heritage and of our living.	—Revelation of God's guidance —Awareness of God as Creator —Ears to hear —God's care about my life —God's love for me —Good news: I have worth	—Authority —Deciding —Answers —Support beyond self —Listening skills —New insights
RESPONDING TO THE WORD: Acting, probing, assimilating the word and words into new patterns of behavior.	—Our role as co-creators —Responsibility —Dialogue —Commitment —Works/faith tied together —Confession/thanks, seeking strength —Work out "salvation"	—Exploring —Taking initiative/choice —Identity/a self-awareness center —Responsibility —Action/response —Finding out answers
AFFIRMING THE COMMUNITY: Saying "yes" to a loving, forgiving life-style	—Our life as God's people —Covenants —Good news/faith as sustainers —The congregation caring for each other —Sharing beliefs and commitments	—A place to belong —"Okayness" —Support/trust/care —Affection —Strength bombardment —Choosing/prizing/cherishing values with others

BIBLE IDEAS THAT DEFINE THIS ORDER	SOME WAYS TO ACT
Isaiah 6, outline for worship Matthew 18:20	—Yell, chant —Music: singing or instrumental —Movements and people shapes —Readings —Getting attention, inviting to respond together
John 1. The living Word Deuteronomy 6:4 "Hear, O Israel" Deuteronomy 11:18-21 Psalms 119, 105	"Now" Testament (current happenings and news) —Singing Scripture —Old and New Testament tied together —Quiet times —Persons sharing "life" stories —Using other senses—seeing; letting creation speak
James 1:23-25 Matthew 13:14-23	—Explore experience/imagination/Bible —Clarify values (Christian) —Self-awareness —Action/not sitting —Put together our own answers —Share stories, differences in understandings —Expressing in other media than verbal (drama, art)
Ephesians 4:25 "Members one of another" 1 Peter 2:9-10. God's people Jeremiah 31:31-34. New covenant. Romans 15:13. Benediction.	—Personal affirmations —Contracting —Ritual benedictions —Promises to care, meet again —Reverence for one another stated —Affirming God/Christ as source of life together

have symbolic richness but is so predictable that it feels flat. I suggest we invent new rituals to meet the needs and particular expressions of our groups. Perhaps we will use a special word or phrase, perhaps a certain act, such as holding hands or hugging, perhaps a repeating of the creations (songs, chants, dramas) that come from special shared events. Try your hand at inventing rituals, or "recycle" some old favorites. Ritual gives order and symbolic richness to remembering and celebrating life.

2. A Case for Silence and Noise!

I disagree with that sign I see in so many sanctuaries: "Silence is required for worship." I guess it must be the "required" that puts me off. I do believe, however, in silence. Just a few experiences with Eastern meditation practices have helped me to realize that Western society talks too much and rarely listens. We're "tellers" of the word, all right. But what about listening, reflection, quiet, being still? Plan some worship that has moments of creative silence, guided meditation, or listening without "telling."

Equally, I'm for "shouts" of joy. Borrow the media of the sports rally squad and create some yells. Yells can be calls to gathering or shouts of thanksgiving or exclamations of joy. Litanies or responsive readings don't have to be mumbled in a monotone! Junior highs have lots of vocal energy. Use it for praising, praying, celebrating. Noise can be JOYFUL NOISE!

3. Self-Interest

As crass as it may sound, self-interest is the major motivator for change. Persons are interested in those things that do most for themselves. Self-affirmation, self-gain, self-recognition—keep these needs in the back of your head when making your plans. Do as much research as you can in the makeup of the "selves" with whom you work. Pitch the involvements and leadership at the level of those self-interests and abilities you know. Positively reinforce the selves and interest, and change has a start. Does this process sound too manipulative? Don't forget that the heart of the good news is that you, yourself, *you* are loved! Our acting out of loving interest in growing/changing selves is the Christian life-style.

BE STILL . . . AND KNOW

PURPOSE

To explore the meaning of quiet and being open to the "messages" of life and creation.

SETTING

This worship event fits any setting, but is especially appropriate for an outdoor place.

METHODS

The methods suggested for this particular worship event are only suggestions. Be flexible and inventive. Some steps may feel inappropriate or awkward for you and your group. Shorten or lengthen, leave out steps, or make additions. Let the methods suggest other ways to you. Use some suggestions in other events and borrow ideas from other spots for this sharing. Worship comes out of life. You and your group must find the best method for you. At the same time, some of the different ideas are a chance for you to risk something new. Take some chance on change. You may be surprised at the response!

ORDER OF WORSHIP

Call to Gathering

A. Sing some hymns and songs to focus the theme on stillness and nature. The leader can refer to the theme in relation to the songs as a way of giving unity to the singing.

B. Assign three or four persons ahead of time to be prepared to give a one-phrase response to the unfinished sentence: "For me, quiet is. . . ." These responses are given after a leader gives a brief (two-sentence) introduction to the worship and the theme. If it is a smaller group, everyone could respond, giving an answer to the sentence. There are no wrong answers; so *all* responses are accepted.

Hearing the Word

A. The leader can invite persons to listen very carefully to the words of the readings and expressions. Ask them to listen with their inner eye and see "images" as the readings are presented.

B. Present the word through the following selections:

1. Read Psalm 46:1-7, 10-11. Here are some options for the presentation of this reading: one person, reading with much interpretation; two persons or two groups reading alternate verses as a chorus; one person reading short phrases dramatically with the listening group repeating the phrase in the same manner in which it was read. Give some careful thought to the way these reading presentations are made. Assign readers in advance so they may prepare. This is an excellent opportunity for junior highs to show or practice leader skills. Use your imagination to invent ways to read, present, and enliven the words of the Bible.

2. Mark 4:9; Ecclesiastes 4:6. An option to accompany this reading is to ask someone, ahead of time, to prepare a drawing to be placed in front of the group as the selection is presented. Elements of the drawing would include: a large ear as the central figure; around the edges, some of the words that bombard the "hearing" of junior high persons (example: friends, grades, winning, freedom, sizes, etc.); superimposed over the center of the picture the words of Psalm 46:10 "Be still, and know. . . ."

3. A reading about friendship:

Friends need each other as listeners. But I have so many things to say, it's hard for me to listen. I have so many questions, it's hard for me to say anything. I feel lonely sometimes, but I'm afraid to ask for your company. I want to be alone sometimes, but I'm afraid to ask you to let me be. I'm sometimes very jealous of you and things you do. I'm sometimes very angry at you. I want to be recognized as best even if it sometimes means I win and you lose. I like you. Can you hear me saying all these mixed-up things? Will you be my listening friend?

4. Read Psalm 8. An option for presenting this psalm is to find a new translation or to rewrite some of the words to correspond to the understandings of your group. For example, with new understanding of the quality of persons, you may consider changing "man" in verse 4 to "what are we," and the "him" to "us." More specifically, you may insert either the name of the group or the names of the persons in the group.

5. Ecology/nature readings: Assign someone to find a short clipping from the local newspaper that reflects concern about nature and natural resources. This can be read as the "now" testament.

6. Singing the Scripture: Ask someone with singing skills to sing short phrases from the Psalm 46 selection. A phrase is sung in "chanting" fashion. The group then sings the phrase, repeating it in the same way as the lead singer.

Responding to the Word

Hearing the word can be dramatic and insightful, but hearing is not enough. We need to be involved in exploring the ideas, pulling out some learnings, comparing our experiences and imagination with the biblical vision and experience. How can persons get involved with the ideas? How can they get their bodies and minds interacting with the expressions? Try these suggestions and invent some of your own. You might even ask the group to plan together and be the inventors!

Invitations to Responding:

A. Slow-motion walk: this is more effective outside but can be done inside. Choose a route and lead the group in a single-file, silent, slow-motion walk. The objective is as follows: to identify with the pilgrims of God who walked in the Way seeking to find the Land of Promise; to be still, in motion and voice, and sense some stillness while slowing the "busyness" of our bodies and inner selves; to "listen" visually, letting the sounds and sights of the surroundings and creation speak. Can a tree speak? Can a person's face say something without words? Can slowing down, breathing deeply, have a message of its own? Explore stillness by walking very slowly, following a particular route to the next spot where the worship will continue.

B. Nonspeaking experiences of listening: When the group arrives at the next spot, the leader will invite them to "be still and listen" in the following ways:

1. Look very carefully at your own hand. What messages does it have? What characteristics of your parents or some work you do does this have? What do the lines and textures and shapes say to you about who you are? What are some hopes for this hand and what it can do?

2. Sitting quietly, take three very deep breaths with your eyes closed. Be inside your self. Hear the "messages" going on inside your head. Feel the messages of your body (breathing, muscles, fidgetiness, silliness—). How does it feel to be quiet? Is it easy? Is it difficult? What helps you to be still? What disrupts the "quiet" in you?

3. Look around you, with stillness. Do the surroundings have a message? Focus on an object (a tree, an insect, a chair, etc.). Imagine it has a voice and can speak to you. Listen to the message and sense the "personality" of the object.

4. Sit in pairs. Look at the other person's face for a while. (Yes, it is hard. You feel like giggling, but try it for thirty seconds.) Use these questions as you look: What feature of the other's face "speaks" to you? Of whom does that person remind you? What do you think the other sees in your face? When you have finished looking, spend a few minutes talking with your partner about what you saw, of whom the other reminded you, what you think the other saw.

5. Share, as a group, about quiet, stillness, listening. Some *options* for discussing are:

a. Use the fishbowl method with part of the group in the center talking, the rest sitting in an outer circle around them, listening. Leave an empty spot for "outside" circle people to enter and make a comment, or let the outside listeners be the inside talkers after a while.

b. Choose a symbol of "speaking." (Any object that can be held in the hand is good.) Only the person holding the symbol may speak. The rest listen. (Remember the conch shell in Golding's novel, *Lord of the Flies*?)

c. Share in small groupings first; then move to the whole group for "reports" of the messages.

d. List some of the messages of the exploring/responding: the hand; inside your self; the walk; objects focused upon; other persons' faces.

Affirming the Community

The group may stand in a circle, close together.

LEADER: We have sung. We have heard. We have explored. We have been still. We have said things with our voices. Let us affirm that we are a listening community. We are a group of people who care enough to hear God's word in creation and to hear each other. May we share the messages with each other. Will you tell us what ideas, learnings, you will be taking away as you leave this place?

INDIVIDUALS:

I will be taking ———————————
     or
I feel ———————————————
     or
I heard ——————————————

GROUP (*after each person speaks*): Be still and know.

Closing: A prayer, an "amen" to the sharing of messages, a moment of quiet, or the chance to mill among friends and say any final private messages as participants go home.

ALL IN THE FAMILY

PURPOSE

To explore and affirm family roots and to identify ourselves as part of the family of God.

ORDER OF WORSHIP

Call to Gathering

A. Naming ourselves: In an opening circle, invite persons to identify their family names. This is done by first proclaiming your own first and middle names and then the names of Mother's and Father's family. Example: "I am Richard Dean, part of the families of Westrom and Orr plus Hutt." (Note: We live in a time when broken families are very prevalent. Allow young persons to affirm and confess this by adding on any extra names related to parent remarriage as additions rather than subtractions. The point is to affirm the person's specialness. This is another "permission giving" tactic related to a delicate emotional subject. Healings of brokenness are part of the "work" of the family of God.)

B. Charting our "family" feelings: Give persons paper and pencil. Have them complete the following chart, sharing one column's instruction at a time. Allow adequate time before moving to the next column. (Note: "Family" can be one person, all the persons in a household, or however the writer interprets it.)

COLUMN 1	COLUMN 2	COLUMN 3	COLUMN 4	COLUMN 5
List 5 good things you get from your family, its "teachings," your family environment.	List some behaviors that make you feel upset about your family.	List some things you hope to do when you are the head of a "family."	List some ways your faith or the church helps you to understand, works with family, or feels like family to you.	List some "if only. . . ."
EXAMPLES: 1. They care about my health, how I look.	1. My brother's noisiness hurts my ears, gives me a headache.	1. I'll have a spot for every person that can be messy or whatever withoug anyone yelling at them to clean it up.	1. Some people listen to me.	1. If only I had my own room. 2. If only the church had "something" for my dad.

Save this chart work for some sharing later in the event. Emphasize that this is private material, that they will not be handing it in to anyone. Any sharing will be only what *they want* to tell.

Hearing the Word

A. The Bible speaks of the "Family of God." The following texts may be used as five short dramatic readings that relate to family and faith:

1 Peter 2:9-10—God's people, belonging
Jeremiah 31:31-34—A new family contract
Galatians 3:26-29—Family unity and diversity
Matthew 18:3-6; 19:14—Love of the child
Luke 15:20-24—The prodigal son, the forgiving father

Some *options* for enhancing the hearing are:
1. Assign a person ahead of time to prepare a brief two- or three-sentence personal statement following each reading. These statements are to be identity

statements. They are meant to give some relation to the Scripture and our here-and-now life.

Example: (following First Peter) "I don't always feel like I belong to anything. I feel, sometimes, like "no people." I do hope for the light of belonging to end the dark, lonely place I sometimes live in."

2. Assign a text to a small group. Ask the group to prepare both a dramatic choral reading of the text and two ideas they get from the text about their families.

3. Write all the texts on newsprint. Invite the whole group to read them aloud in unison.

4. Assign persons before the session to bring in clippings from local newspapers about "family." Some of these may be read as part of the word, perhaps even correlated with the texts.

Responding to the Word

A. Sharing family charts: In small groups, no more than three, invite persons to share what they see in the charts they did above in the "Gathering." Are there similarities in the columns? What patterns do they see in their attitudes across the columns? What seems most important to them in the whole chart? This sharing is to help them identify similar feelings with one another. They may, however, be willing to prepare one "I learned . . ." statement from their chart that they would share with the group.

B. Family collages: Divide into two groups. With magazines, scissors, paste, and newsprint, invite one group to cut out pictures of positive family values; the other group is to cut out pictures they feel emphasize negative family values. Make composite pictures of these value choices. Share the products; make observations; share feelings.

C. Family discussions: For each of the statements below choose four speakers. Two speakers are affirmative; two are negative about the statement. Each speaker speaks for two minutes. When both sets of four speakers have finished, use a small fishbowl discussion (four to six persons in the middle talking, the rest as listeners). The fishbowl group will work on the topic: Can the family teach us how to be Christian persons? The debate statements are:

1. "There is no such thing as a Christian family."

2. "The family that prays together stays together." Conclude this discussion period by asking persons to express some hopes about Christian faith and family living.

D. Family pictures: Ask persons to draw a relationship diagram of their family. One way to do this is to draw a diagram of the family dinner table as they felt it when they were age ten. Place persons around the table in the relation they were to each other. Draw colored and shaped lines to indicate the communication patterns. Invite persons to share their diagrams in the whole group or in groups of five with an adult leader.

An interesting option would be to invite each person to bring a real family picture. A person could then tell the story of each family member and describe their communication relation.

Affirming the Community

A. Sing the "Community" song by Robert Blue on the F.E.L. record, "Run, Come, See." (Order from: F.E.L. Publications, Ltd., 1925 Pontius Ave., Los Angeles, CA 90025.) Or use another song about being together.

B. New behavior reports: Ask persons to share any intentions they have about their home family. Let them state one specific behavior they want to try. Affirm these reports with a celebrative cheer.

C. Read again 1 Peter 2:9-10; ask three persons, ahead of time, to offer short prayers of hope and support for the families of this group.

WAITING FOR THE GIFT

PURPOSE

To explore and experience feelings about Christmas and its "personal" gifts.

ORDER OF WORSHIP

Call to Gathering

A. Before persons arrive, put around the room four or five pictures or posters without words. Pictures can be of scenery, people, or art prints. Next to each put a large piece of paper. As the persons arrive, invite them each to take a crayon or felt-tip pen and write their own Christmas card captions for each picture.

B. When all are present, begin by standing in front of each card in turn and ask each person to read aloud the caption he or she has written. An option would be to ask one reader to read all the captions for one card.

C. As a whole group, or in smaller groups, sit in a circle. Let each person share a major anticipation feeling they have about Christmas. What do you most "wait" for?

Hearing the Word

A. Assign a person or persons ahead of time to read the story of the wise men from Matthew 2:1-12. An exciting option would be to invite a small group of junior highs to prepare a dramatic "telling" of the story of the Magi. Storytelling, when well done, is still one of the finest ways to communicate. With all sorts of media available to us, we have many options. Some of the more simple possibilities are:

1. Record the story, with two or three narrators, on a cassette tape including contemporary background music.

2. Create contemporary pictures to go along with the ancient story by doing one of the following: cut and mount pictures from magazines; draw your illustrations of key sequences; act out the story while the narrator "tells"; take pictures or slides (early enough to develop!) of scenes and persons from your town which might illustrate the meanings of the story and relate it to your space.

3. Tell the story and include persons from outside the youth group but from the church who might appear as "guest speakers." These "guests" would play contemporary versions of the Magi. They would create a "history" and a "purpose for going on the trip" for each Magi which they would report during the telling. Don't be stuck with the old wise "man" motif. Perhaps your Magi should include women!

Tell the story interspersed with the singing of verses of contemporary hymns and songs. The songs could be chosen to fit the moods and phrases of the story. For example, sing "Morning Has Broken" as travelers begin, "He's Got the Whole World in His Hands" as they leave.

Responding to the Word

Some experiences to get people involved and experiencing the waiting and the feeling of the Magi might be:

A. In small groups, do research from a Bible dictionary on Magi, frankincense, myrrh, manger, Bethlehem (and anything else relating to the Advent story). Invite the research teams to give reports of their major findings to the group.

B. Be modern Magi. Invite persons to sense themselves as gift-bringers to the baby Jesus. This is a sort of "drama" in which every person creates a self-role. The role is created by giving persons about ten minutes time to:

1. Choose a new name to fit your identity as a "wise one." Tell what gift you bring. The gift should be something you feel is a real skill that you could offer to

the group and the world. Examples: "I am Hermes. I bring the gift of understanding numbers." "I am Ear-Able. I bring the gift of listening."

2. Do the sharing of new names and the gifts brought to society for *this* time. Note these carefully and affirm them. They are very important expressions of the selves. Allow each person to talk about his or her gift and permit questions to be asked. (The permission-giving of this tactic is taking the roles and being, for a moment, another person. An important part of leading is giving persons regular permission to be all the specialness they really are!)

C. Have a Christmas tree: This is a relational game. The leader "becomes" the magic Christmas tree. The rules by which the tree offers its gifts are:

1. Gifts requested must be self-generating and relate to emotional needs of the seeker.

2. Gifts must be "paid for" with emotional qualities the seeker feels as extra strength.

The tree talks with the seekers one at a time, in front of the group. The seeker makes a request for some emotional "gift." To repeat, the gift sought must be something that can be responsibly developed by the individual. For example, a person may not request "respect" because that quality depends upon others. The quality that generates respect from others which does come from inside the self is self-appreciation. In terms of faith this is appropriate because the "good news" is news of love, forgiveness, and acceptance.

An example of a transaction with the magic tree would be: The seeker requests "five pounds" of patience with brothers and sisters. The tree interviews the seeker a bit to clarify the need and use of the patience. The seeker agrees to "pay" with "two gallons" of "crazy imagination." Part of the negotiation is discovering the "quality" of these goods and the percentage the seeker is willing to give away of the supply. The game is serious and real needs are expressed, but it should be done in a spirit of comic drama and with lots of frivolous fun!

When transactions are finished, talk about the giving-receiving of emotional "gifts" and the Christmas event.

Affirming the Community

A. Play or sing a carol about the coming "Gift." "What Child Is This?" or "O Come, O Come, Emmanuel" would be appropriate.

B. Share prayers of hope, either in a sentence fashion or in the following ritual:

INDIVIDUAL: I hope the Child coming brings _____.
GROUP RESPONSE: We live in hope!

C. A closing chant: The leader says the lines (or assigns them to individuals ahead of time). The group repeats the lines together.

Holy Child, we wait your coming.
We bring gifts of self, and hope.
Bring us gifts.
Bring us inside-feeling-goodness.
Bring us forgiving more than once.
Bring us friend-being skills.
We live, waiting, in hope!
Amen, Amen!

CHOOSE LIFE

PURPOSE

To explore choosing as a central faith issue.

A THEOLOGICAL NOTE

There are two basic belief assumptions of the author that underlie this particular topic. They undergird some of the suggestions, but they, as beliefs, need not be affirmed in order for this material to be useful to you.

> "We are co-creators, *with* God, of our life-style."
> (This does not at all mean equality with God; it just means we've got something to say about our life, too!)

> "We are responsible for the quality of our life."
> (This is a stewardship/"clean up after yourself" comment.)

ORDER OF WORSHIP

Call to Gathering

A. Play the song "Free to Be" from the Ms. recording "Free to Be You and Me." If it's unavailable, select another contemporary song that deals with choosing. Put the words on newsprint for singing or reading.

B. Introduce the idea of choosing. On a piece of newsprint or chalkboard, in brainstorm fashion, list all the kinds of decisions or choices that persons in this group have had to make in the last seven days. Example: The decision whether to make one's bed in the morning or leave it. Then list as many feelings about making these choices as persons can identify. Example: frustrated, relieved, etc.

C. Use the "feeling" words in an opening call to worship. For example, the leader reads; the group repeats.

We come from many homes.
We try to understand living and being.
Daily, we face choosing,
   deciding.
   separating,
   either this or that,
   for and against.
   choosing!
Our choosing feels: *(read together "feeling" list from above.)*
Lord of our living, help us to choose life!

Hearing the Word

A. Read aloud together, in dramatic style, Deuteronomy 30:19; Micah 6:8; Joshua 24:14-15; Matthew 6:24.

B. Ask a group, ahead of time, to create new song words to an old tune on the theme "choosing." Sing this as part of the hearing.

Responding to the Word

A. *A role play:* Ask three persons to be "choosers." The choosers enter the room without announcement as soon as the opening is finished. Each of them picks a person from the group to whom they deliver the following assignment lines:

1. "You have been chosen to be president of the United States. These people in this room are your Congress. They must decide, in ten minutes, about a crucial law. The law decrees that all families in America will pay $100 in extra taxes this year to be used by the United Nations to feed hungry people wherever they are. You must give Congress a recommendation. The recommendation must include what you believe their decision should be and two reasons for that decision."

2. "You are a brain surgeon. The people in this

room are your staff. They must make a choice in ten minutes about a serious surgery. The patient is a fifteen-year-old young woman with a brain tumor. She is a well-known tennis player who could become professional. If the tumor is not removed, she will be paralyzed from the waist down and will not walk. If the tumor is removed, she has a good chance of walking; but the operation is so delicate that she may die. Your staff needs your recommendation and two reasons why you recommend a particular decision."

3. "You have been chosen leader of this group with the power to make decisions for the group. You have declared that you will consult the group on all decisions. You must make an important decision because the group is trapped in a cave with only a twenty-four-inch hole carved in rock to climb out. There is a good possibility that only one person will get out. You, with your group, must decide who the person will be. In ten minutes the group wants your recommendations and two reasons why."

Process. The persons chosen go out of the room for ten minutes to work out their recommendations. If there are enough people, those who "chose" them may go with them as consultants. While they are gone, the rest of the group divides itself into three work groups. Each group will work with one of the "chosen." The job of the group is to hear the recommendation, make a group decision, and report it to the whole group. (This may sound as if it demands a large youth group, but the fact is that six persons could conduct this exploration.) Groups must be as equal in number as possible, and there should be at least one member of each sex.

Members should form themselves into the three groups in five minutes, so they have five minutes to talk as a group about the decisions they may make.

When those delegated return, they work with their groups for ten to fifteen minutes. They share their recommendations, and the group seeks to make a consensus decision. This may involve some compromises and conditions so that the whole group can agree. They must make some kind of decision to report at the end of the stated time.

Reports are given, and the whole group then debriefs the deciding process. Talk about:

1. How did the delegates feel?

2. What were the problems in making a good decision?

3. What seemed to help you most to make a decision? (This is a question for the whole group.)

4. What sort of process did your work group use to make a decision? (Include how they decided which group to work in!)

5. What are some things we can learn about decision making from this experience?

B. *Some alternatives to option A:*

1. *Bible choices:* Look at some Bible stories together. Discuss the decisions/choices that seemed to be made. Choose some of the stories and invite two persons to act them out with the same questions but coming to a "different" decision than the one presented in the story. Some possible stories are:

    a. Jesus and the woman: John 8:3-11.

    b. Judas, accepting the bribe: Luke 22:3-6.

    c. Moses' mother, deciding to put him in the river: Exodus 2:3.

    d. Jesus and the paralyzed man: Luke 5:17-20.

    e. Jesus and the rich young ruler: Matthew 19:16-22.

    f. Peter, at the first denial; Matthew 26:69-70.

After the "plays," compare the consequences of the original decision and the "new" decision. Talk about consequences as part of the choosing process.

2. *Self-choosing:* rank the following decisions one through eight in terms of difficulty in deciding. One is the most difficult; eight is the easiest.

    a. Leaving home to live alone.

    b. Changing the color of your hair.

    c. Telling a boy/girl friend you no longer want to go steady.

    d. Stopping all your yelling and anger outbursts at home.

    e. Learning how to do something you have never tried before.

    f. Refusing drugs/alcohol from a close friend.

    g. Learning you can never have any children of your own.

    h. Being active at church.

Talk about your choices with a small group. Can you identify what value motivates how you choose?

3. *Describe five qualities you would like to have as a self.* Beside each quality write one thing you're going to "choose" to do to work toward that quality. As a group define five outstanding qualities of "someone" (each person can think of a different someone) who is a model of Christian life-style to you. Compare these to the qualities you originally chose.

Affirming the Community

A. Read Joshua 24:14-15 again.

B. Make some "I learned . . ." statements about choosing.

C. Repeat the chant from the "Call to Gathering" as a closing prayer.

CLOSING NOTES AND OBSERVATIONS ABOUT WORSHIP

WORSHIP IS LEARNING, TOO!

As you can observe, these events are based on the philosophy that worship includes education. Isn't the sermon a teaching-learning event? So the worship event is a learning/exploring activity. These events are only one set of suggestions. Enhance these topics with your own materials: readings, songs, forms. Let your style of exploring and learning together be the forms of worship.

JUNIOR HIGHS CAN CREATE

Encourage and accept creativity. Worship has no "right" way. Keep up the invitation to invent. Give lots of "permission." Make specific assignments to create. Believe your group can do it!

INTERGENERATIONAL ACTIVITIES

These suggestions are okay for a broad range of ages. Consider the possibility of the junior highs sponsoring a six-week elective with the senior adults on "Saying Yea: New Ways to Worship." Invite parents and other adults to be leaders and participants in these events.

WHAT IS WORSHIP, ANYWAY?

There are lots of tentative answers to that question. Some of them assert lots of rightness! But dialogue is needed. Keep working on it. Keep thinking. The issue is not settled. You can contribute to the research.

Accept the following reading as a closing affirmation of one person's faith/life. Let us continue to struggle together with the meanings of worship and learning.

Come, O Come, Emmanuel.
Invite health to my feeling
                    broken
                    spot.
Come, Creator of light and dark.
Invite stillness to the quivering
                    fear
                    spot.
Come, Revealer of the way.
Put my feet and being in
            steps
            that
            feel firm,
                festive,
                fertile . . .
Come, O Come, little Babe.
        Restore
        play and innocence,
    a way of seeing
                surprise!
Come, Inviter of healing.
    Give me muscles
        to carry
        my beds of paralysis,
    to climb down from trees,
    to go home and live.
Be here, Spirit of growing,
        Enabler of caring,

WALK IN THE WAY WITH US!

Rev. Richard D. Orr is director of the American Baptist Center, Kansas University, Lawrence, Kansas.

SECTION III
Leadership Resources

SURVIVING AS AN ADULT ADVISOR

by ROBERT G. MIDDLETON, JR.

You may have just said "yes" to the telephone caller, and suddenly you realize that you have agreed to serve as the junior high sponsor in your church for an indefinite period. Or, you may have said "yes" several years ago and have been having a fairly good experience. Whichever category you belong in, one of the most common and frustrating areas in your job may be finding support in your job. Who can you talk to about what happened at last Sunday's meeting? Who will be as enthusiastic as you about the changes and growth that have been and are taking place in yourself and individuals in the group?

These and other questions and their accompanying frustrations have been asked since the beginning of youth ministry—and they will no doubt continue to be asked in the years ahead. There are really no hard and fast answers to these questions, but there are some suggestions which might be tossed out. They are only suggestions and must be checked against your own experience and needs.

DON'T TRY TO DO IT ALONE!

Even if you are the only adult who works with the junior high group on a regular basis, you will be much more effective and feel better about yourself and what you are doing if you have someone with whom you can share ideas or talk about joys and frustrations. The ideal is to have two or more (depending on the size of your group) adults who work together on a regular basis with the group. If this is your case, you are fortunate to have part of the question of support licked. This team, if it works right, can be a source of support to one another and can illustrate to the members of the junior high group that the church is concerned about them and wants to provide a good experience for them.

Another excellent reason for having a team approach to junior high ministry is that the large amount of time which is required to do an adequate job in youth ministry can be divided between the adults. No one, whether a professional or lay person, really has enough time to do all that is required—phoning, meeting with the group or individuals, researching possible programs, etc. By utilizing the team approach, the time required by any one member is not so overwhelming.

The team approach also offers the opportunity for developing closer relationships with the youth in your group. Instead of having to relate to a total group, you can begin to look at individuals in the group and become more aware of their particular needs and abilities. As with any other human being, junior highs are going to find it easier to relate to some people than others. A team approach allows this to happen—in fact, it encourages it.

SUPPORT FROM THE CHURCH

Even if you are fortunate enough to work in a team ministry, there is still a need for others in the church to support those who are doing ministry with youth. Education policy boards or committees should become involved by helping to set goals for youth ministry in the church and by evaluating the progress being made toward reaching these goals.

Perhaps the most important group in the church with whom youth advisors may relate is a youth committee composed of interested and concerned adults who on a fairly regular basis can meet with the advisors to talk about specific areas of concern and celebrate areas of joy. This group can either be formally designated by the educational policy board or be an ad-hoc group formed because of its interest in youth ministry. Whatever is the case, this group can prove to be invaluable in assisting you, the advisor, in carrying out your ministry. And surrounding all of this must be the congregation, committed to a ministry with youth that will enable them to grow and develop as full human beings. Without this kind of commitment on the part of the whole church, youth ministry will struggle along in its own world, providing experiences for the youth, but never really affirming the part which youth play in the total ministry of the church.

REACHING JUNIOR HIGHS

On a different level, but of equal importance, is the support and guidance you as an adult can give to the junior high young person. Even as you need support in order to do your job, so, too, the junior high needs to know that there are adults to whom he or she can turn for guidance and support. The junior high young person is going through one of the most crucial and frustrating times in development. No longer looked upon as children, yet not quite old enough to be independent, the junior highs are thrust into an unknown world, unsure who they are or what is expected of them. Consequently, junior highs need to know that there are some adults who can be turned to in time of need.

Setting Limits. Junior highs, because of this uncertainty in knowing themselves, are constantly testing the limits, seeing how far they can go in their behavior. This means the adult leader must establish and enforce limits on their behavior—limits which allow the junior highs enough freedom to experiment and move out beyond themselves, but provide enough structure so that the youth are not left completely to their own resources. As the adult leader, your task in this area is not an easy one. Some junior highs can handle more freedom than others—some groups need a very rigid set of rules under which they operate. No two individuals or groups are alike. Your main responsibility is to determine how much freedom can be given your group which allows them to perform at their best. A word of warning: What worked well one week may not necessarily work the next week. Your group can change its character, depending on things that have happened during the week—so be prepared to be flexible and ready to adapt.

One further word—you, as a person, have needs, too. While you want to provide the best environment possible for the youth, make certain it is within your own personal limits, too. If your needs and those of the group are incompatible, it may be time for you to move to another area of work in the church. But usually a working arrangement can be arrived at to the benefit of you and the group.

INTERPRETING TO PARENTS

An important group for you to relate to in some way—both for your sake and also for the well-being of the group—is the parents. This group is often overlooked as a valuable aid in the church's ministry with youth. Communication between you and the parents of youth can be one of the most important areas of involvement you have outside your contact with the group. Parents can make your job much easier or they can make it miserable. The amount of communication you have with them can make the difference.

There are several ways communication can be maintained without involving a great deal of extra time on your part. One is simply to publish a listing, with times and dates, of known activities in which your group will be involved. This would include such things as time and location of regular meetings, retreats or overnight events, special parties or outings, and any other activities in which your group might be involved. Doing this helps parents feel that they at least have some idea of what will be happening to their young person, and they can plan accordingly.

Some churches have found it very helpful to have a meeting or meetings of parents and advisors where each can share ideas and suggestions can be made. This approach might be very beneficial at the beginning and perhaps again in the middle and near the end of the program year. This allows parents to feel that their views are important and that they have some say in the direction the youth group will be going. But perhaps more importantly, it allows you, as the youth advisor, to enlist their support for what you have planned. With that knowledge, a parent can be a tremendous asset to you and your program.

William H. R. Willkens, in his book *The Youth Years,* said:

It is impossible to overestimate the importance of the home in the development of a vital faith in young people, because the roots of their faith go back through childhood and grow in the midst of parental guidance and example. In the home atmosphere the faith of young people is nourished by the general spiritual climate of the home and through many experiences, such as:

—sharing in family planning and decision-making
—responsible participation in the conduct of the home
—discussions on the meaning of life and the place of religious faith in dealing with problems
—the use of prayer in the home
—family traditions in the celebration of Christmas and other religious holidays
—attendance together at church worship services and at other activities for study and fellowship
—family concern for others, demonstrated in discussions and in

projects of service and sharing through church and community agencies.[1]

Dr. Willken's message is unmistakably clear to all who work with youth—parents and parental support are vital to the program you as a youth advisor are trying to build. You can't do your job alone, and you can't do it without the active support and input of parents.

HOW MUCH TIME?

A question you need to ask yourself is: How much of my time do I want to give to youth ministry and what other types of involvements do I need to have as a person and a member of this church? While the job you have agreed to—namely, being an advisor to a youth group—should be your first priority, there may be other areas in the life of the church where you feel you want to be involved. If you can do this and still feel you can devote adequate time and energy to youth ministry—go ahead.

WHAT ARE YOU EXPECTED TO DO?

What Do You Say After You Say Hello? is the title of a current book being widely read now. The title sums up many of the anxieties and fears a youth advisor faces when going into a group of junior highers. "What will I do with them?" "How will they respond to me?" These and similar questions run through the minds of all youth advisors. So don't feel like an odd-ball if you have them! The real trick is to confront your anxieties and questions and deal with them. Some of them will never be overcome, which is fine. You should be a little nervous meeting with your group. But don't allow your nervousness to inhibit you from action. Listed below are some ideas you may have already tried or may want to attempt with your group.

1. Do some advance planning

Don't wait until the day before the group is to meet to come up with a program. If possible, plan for two or more months in advance so you have some ideas of what you will be working on with the group. You may have to revise or completely throw away some programs because the needs of your group have changed, but this is much better than waiting until the last minute to do the initial planning.

Planning ahead also allows you to develop a theme

[1]William H. R. Willkens, *The Youth Years* (Valley Forge: Judson Press, 1967), pp. 140-141. Used by permission.

and carry it through. This can be very helpful for junior highs who need to feel they have participated in something from its conception to its completion. By planning ahead, you can also involve the young people in more of the planning process, thus giving them a real feeling of participation in the life of their group.

2. Be yourself with the group

Have a good time and let the junior highs know (more by how you act than what you say) that you enjoy being with them. A group that knows their leader would rather be doing something else is going to respond in ways which are detrimental to the group's growth and development. Remember that the young people are looking for an adult to whom they can respond as a friend, as someone to whom they feel close. They can't do this if you remain aloof from them.

3. Not all meetings of the group have to be content-centered

Junior highs are at a very active age—trying out new roles, different forms of behavior. Their week can be fairly structured and "pressurized." The time for your youth group meeting might be a time when they need the opportunity to let their hair down and have fun. Playing together can be beneficial, and in some cases more beneficial to the health of a group than a series of serious meetings. Plan some activities where the only purpose is to be together and have a good time. Some groups plan a meeting like this at least once a month. Others do it at different intervals. Whatever the schedule, plan some fun activities with your group.

4. If possible, do some things with other churches

It's exciting for the junior highs to plan and carry out an activity where they host another group. Members of your group are not isolated from other youth—they see them in school; they play with them. It can be a very worthwhile experience to have two or more churches get together at various times for meetings and/or activities.

5. Take your group on overnight outings and retreats

It is always exciting for a junior high young person to get away from home and spend a length of time with others. In addition, it affords you, the leader, a chance to spend time with members of the group, getting to know them in a different setting. More can probably be accomplished in one weekend retreat than in two months of weekly meetings.

6. Most important of all—STAY FLEXIBLE!

Always be prepared to scrap what you have planned. Your group changes from week to week, and thus their needs will be different. Don't try to push something on the group which it isn't prepared to accept. It is much better to back off and do something else than to ram a program through.

7. Evaluation is of the utmost necessity

Without evaluating what you have done, there is no base upon which to project for the future. You need to do some personal evaluation about your feelings as an advisor—how you see yourself in the group, how you feel about the group and its attitude and direction. If you work in a team effort, these evaluations need to be checked out with the other members of the team—and theirs with you. If possible, sit down with your pastor and/or youth committee or educational policy committee and get their feedback and input.

Evaluation is one of the areas we sometimes gloss over in our desire to move to the next phase of planning, but it is the beginning point of all really constructive planning. With good evaluation, new directions for programming will become very evident. Without it, you will be running around in circles accomplishing very little except increasing your load of frustrations. So set aside a block of time for your personal and team evaluation as one of the first things you do in your youth ministry.

WHERE TO FIND TRAINING

While experience is the best trainer for working with your particular group, everyone needs to refresh him/herself periodically and gain new insights and ideas on ways of working with youth groups. For a person just beginning as an advisor, training can make the first few exposures to the group much less painful and traumatic.

Most denominations offer some training experiences for youth workers, either nationally or regionally. In addition, a number of nondenominational organizations offer training sessions in a wide variety of fields. As an advisor, you should try to avail yourself of these opportunities as your schedule permits. If your church doesn't allocate money for these conferences and workshops, try to have them include this in future planning.

FINDING RESOURCES

All resources, including this book, need to be examined critically. Just because someone has written a program, and outlined how it is to be done, does not mean that you can use it as is. Keep *your* group in mind and adapt resource material to work with your group—not vice versa. All printed resources are done for mass consumption and will not automatically fit your particular situation. So read them over, get your ideas, and make your own plans on how to do a given program.

Above all, as you involve yourself in youth ministry—have fun! Don't look on it as an obligation that must be fulfilled—look on it as an opportunity for you to grow and for the young people you work with to develop into the fullness of being that God intended for them.

Robert G. Middleton, Jr., is a minister of the First Baptist Church, West Hartford, Connecticut.

SECTION IV
RECREATION
RESOURCES

JUNIOR HIGH RECREATION

Some Guidelines

Recreation is an important part of ministry with junior highs. Whether it is an organized hike, bike trip, softball game, or simply a party in someone's basement or games in the church recreation room, good recreation provides opportunities for:

• junior highs to get to know each other better; to feel at ease with others in the group.

• adults to "let their hair down" and let the "child" within them communicate with junior highs on a nonthreatening, fun level.

• both junior highs and adults to become "real" to each other.

• physical activity that lets off the steam that builds up as junior highs face the pressures of adolescence.

• breathing space for junior highs; a chance for them to relax and rebuild their strength.

To do all of these things, however, certain things must be kept in mind while planning.

1. *Don't plan too many competitive activities.* Junior highs are very sensitive to the pressure of both peers and parents to perform well in competitive situations. And often their bodies are developing too fast for them to have the physical control necessary for good athletic performance. So, recreation which is competitive makes them tense rather than relaxing them as it should. When they fail to perform well, they develop unhealthy feelings about themselves. If you use competitive sports at all, make sure teams are evenly matched and provide a "debriefing" time after every game when junior highs can deal with their feelings about their performance.

2. *Encourage junior highs to plan their own recreation.* It is surprising to some adults to discover that "parlor games" they played as children are still popular with junior highs, or to discover that some new game has become a fad at the local junior high school. By involving junior highs in planning their own recreation, you will make certain that the plans are relevant.

3. *Provide a variety of recreational activities.* The focus on team sports in the public school has excluded many young teens from finding recreational outlets. The church can remedy this situation by providing a variety of recreational options. Some youth like table games; some like to hike by themselves; some like to play tennis; some like bowling or roller-skating or hockey. Encourage members of the group to "do their

own thing," and to try new things. Don't push everyone to do the same thing at the same time.

4. *Don't look at recreation as an "extra."* Recreation should be an integral part of your junior high ministry—not an extra. It is as important to offer times of relaxation and fun as it is to offer times for serious study or quiet worship.

5. *Recognize that some youth may only be interested in recreation.* Some churches complain that they can get fifty junior highs out for a roller-skating party and only ten out for a study group on Sunday night. This is not hard to explain. Just as some adults are not ready for serious study of the Christian faith but enjoy being with other people in the church, some junior highs need the chance to test the junior high group in an informal, noncommitment situation. They may be drawn into a closer relationship with the group later. But even if this doesn't happen, you have ministered to their recreational needs.

6. *Relax and enjoy yourself.* For recreation to be fun for the whole group, you, as leader, must learn not to take it too seriously. If you are playing a silly game, act silly. If you are responsible for twenty bikers on a bike hike, make certain the hike has been planned well enough in advance that you can enjoy it.

RESOURCES FOR RECREATION

The New Pleasure Chest by Helen and Larry Eisenberg. (Nashville: Abingdon Press, 1975). $3.95.
Recreation for Retarded Teenagers and Young Adults by Bernice W. Carlson and David R. Ginglend. (Nashville: Abingdon Press, 1968). $4.95.

PARTIES

Recreation at junior high parties often takes the form of "parlor games." These games provide enough structure for young teens to relate to each other without feeling tongue-tied and embarrassed, and are enough fun that they relax junior highs and help them enjoy themselves in a social situation that, for many of them, could be awkward.

The following pages suggest party games for several different occasions. Mix and match these suggestions for parties planned by your own junior high group.

PARTY

by LESLIE E. DUNKIN

WOULD YOU LIKE to make new friends of all the new faces that have appeared in your Fellowship this fall? Ask them "Who are you?" in this party and you're well on your way. While you're at it, you may be surprised at what you discover about old friends you thought you knew!

INVITATIONS

Draw a large question-mark on folded white or colored paper. Print "W H O" in the curve at the top, "R" at the lower left and "U?" at the lower right. It will look like this:

Inside the folder print the invitation as follows: We'd like to find out, so come to _____ on _____ at _____ o'clock.

THE PARTY

Greetings

As your guests arrive, give each a numbered name tag. It should have a line stating "I Am ____ ____". Below this there should be a "Who R U?" question mark like the one on the invitations. Direct each person to write his or her first and last name in the blank and then introduce himself or herself to five other guests.

Vital Statistics

Give each guest a slip of paper that calls for the following personal information: number of teeth, head measure, length of nose, distance from fingertip to fingertip with outstretched arms, weight of hand, size of big toe, and any other valuable statistics.

Scales, yardsticks, and tape measures should be used, with someone in charge of each to register the correct figures.

Have each person write his or her name on the paper. Then collect them and remind the guests not to tell any of their personal information.

Glad-Hand Welcome

Seat your guests in two groups, the even numbers and the odds. (Numbers are on the name tags which were given out as guests arrived.) Line up the even numbers and have the odd numbers pass by them, shake hands with each, and note the name of each hand-shaking friend.

The "odds" will then go into an adjoining room with a drapery or heavy blanket covering the doorway. One by one they will stick only their hand through an opening in the door covering. One of the "evens" will shake it and guess whose it is. A point is awarded for each correct guess. Reverse the two groups to let the "odds" guess the "evens." The group with the highest total of points wins.

Throwing Weight Around

Let the losing Glad-Hand group select two of their members and challenge the other group to guess which two of their members have the same total hand weight. If the guess is within two ounces, the guessers will earn a point and will select another two to match two from the other group. If a combination is not matched within two ounces, the challenging side is awarded a point. They then challenge the other team again with two different members.

To check the weight combinations, the leader of the game will consult the registration slips and add the hand weights of each pair.

After one side has earned five consecutive points the other side will automatically be given a chance to make a challenge.

The group with the larger total when time is called wins.

Headway

Each group will select a "head." This person will stand with hands held behind the back, while the other members of that group toss from a distance a man's felt hat. The "head" may move the head, but not the feet or hands, to assist in catching the hat. Each member of the group will get one try. A point is given each time the hat is tossed onto the head. The group with the largest total of "head" points wins.

Who Are You?

Give each guest a pencil and sheet of paper. In numbered order, read the vital statistics from the slips that were filled out earlier without giving the name of the individual. Everyone should guess who each vital statistic belongs to, and write the name on their paper opposite the number called. A point will be granted for each one guessed correctly. The winner will be the one with the largest total of points.

Let's Eat!

Have half of the group toss their name tags into a hat. Then have a drawing for the other half. Each person will eat with the person whose name he or she draws.

If you can find small candy canes, somewhat the shape of a question mark, have one for each guest. Cookies baked in this shape might be used instead. Regular cookies might have icing in the shape of the question mark. A gelatin fruit salad can be served with whipped cream on top in the shape of the party's question mark.

Urge your guests to find out all they can about the person with whom they are eating.

After refreshments, have a "sing along" time with fun songs that are popular with your group.

APRIL FOOLISH FUN

by ERMA REYNOLDS

ON APRIL FOOL'S DAY, when folks have their mind on fooling and foolery, why not invite your fellowship to have some April Foolish Fun?

INVITATIONS

Write out invitations backwards on light cardboard. They will have to be held up to a mirror in order to be read.

DECORATIONS

Decorate the room with April fool tricks. Place bouquets of flowers on which black pepper has been sprinkled on several tables. Hang a toy mouse from the ceiling. Glue a real coin to the floor. Post foolish signs and mottos on the walls.

SILLY STUNTS

Nose Wriggle

Before the party, cut gummed labels into small squares, about postage stamp size, with one for each guest. To start the foolish fun, divide the gang into two groups and have them stand in lines, facing each other. Have each player wet one of the gummed squares on his or her tongue and then paste this firmly onto the tip of his or her nose. When all are decorated with labels, instruct them to wiggle the label off their noses without any use of their hands. Between watching the frantic efforts of one's neighbors, and wriggling one's own nose, everyone is sure to get mighty silly over this stunt.

Balloon Race

Tie an inflated balloon to the ankle of each player. It is then up to the players to break the balloons of the other players, and at the same time try to keep their own balloon from being broken. The last player left with a whole balloon wins. This is a dilly of a silly contest to watch, so players won't mourn too much when their broken balloon puts them out of the running.

Nut in the Bottle

Bring out three sturdy chairs. Three persons play this game at one time, while the others watch their foolish antics. On the floor behind each chair, place three long-necked bottles. Each of the three players receives a piece of string about seven feet long, with a shell peanut tied to one end. At the starting signal the contestants mount their chairs, facing its back. They place the end of the string in their mouth and set to work to maneuver the peanut into the bottle. This is done by chewing up the string and guiding the nut into the bottle. Their foolish facial contortions are certain to have the watching guests laughing their heads off. The first player to land the nut in the bottle wins. Then, three more players take their places on the chairs and carry out the same procedure. When everyone has had a turn, the winners of each set demand a foolish forfeit from their defeated opponents.

Why and Because

This is a game old enough to show white whiskers, but it can still hold its own for foolish fun. Give each player a pencil and two slips of paper. On one slip they write a silly question which begins with the word "why." Collect these slips in a paper bag and shake them up thoroughly. On the second slip the players write the answer to their question, beginning the sentence with the word "because." These slips go into a second bag and are also given a shake to mix. Each person in turn draws a slip from each bag and reads aloud the question followed by the answer. Needless to say, the results from this blind drawing are foolish.

Counting Marbles

Divide into small groups of four persons. Place a shallow dish filled with marbles in the center of the floor. Give each person in the first group of four players a foolish face mask, pie-tin, and a teaspoon. Instruct them to put on their "foolish face" and kneel upright on the floor, about two feet away from the dish of marbles. At the starting signal they place their pie-tin against their forehead and proceed to pick up marbles one at a time with the teaspoon, depositing

132

them in their pie-tin. Should a marble drop enroute, it must be run down by the player and picked up with the spoon without using the fingers to work the marble back into the spoon. When all of the marbles have been taken from the middle dish, the players count the marbles they landed in their pie-tin, and the player with the most marbles wins the round. Then, four more players take over the equipment and carry out the contest in the same fashion. When everyone has had a turn, the winners compete against each other to determine the grand winner. This is another silly dilly contest to watch.

REFRESHMENTS

Serve refreshments backwards. Begin with cakes, then serve sandwiches, and finish with a light gelatin salad.

FISHING FUN PARTY

by JUNE STAFFORD

When Simple Simon went a-fishing to catch a whale, all the water he could get was in his mother's pail. Like Simple Simon, most of the water we have for our Fishing Fun Party will be in a pail. However, spirits won't be dampened in the least at this fun fest.

INVITATIONS

Cut fish shapes from green art paper. In black crayon make scales and other details of a fish. On the back write the invitation:
    Come bring your line and sinkers
    Your reel and fish-hooks too.
    We're having a Fishing Fun Party.
    It starts at half-past two.
Host _____ Place _____

DECORATIONS

For the centerpiece use fish net with cardboard anchors and fish hooks inserted here and there. If desired, glass Japanese net balls may be added to the net.

Cut-outs of fish may be placed throughout the play area.

ICE BREAKER

Before guests arrive, make several large cardboard fish and cut into pieces like a jigsaw puzzle. Give each guest one piece as he or she arrives. When all guests have helped to put the fish together, you are ready to start the next game.

WHALES IN PAILS

Tie a long kite string on a bamboo pole or other stick of fishpole length. Attach a small magnet to the free end of the string.

Cut a number of paper fish and attach paper clips, hair pins, or a similar object that will be attracted by the magnet.

Place fish in a large shallow pan. Let each guest take a turn trying to catch one of Simple Simon's whales.

FISHTAIL HOP (RELAY RACE)

Divide players into two teams, the Cods and the Soles. Mark a line for the starting point at one end of the play area and another line about four feet away.

At a signal, the leaders from each team hop fish fashion to the farthest line and back to tap the next in line. (Fish fashion: Heels are placed together, toes apart, representing a fish tail.)

SCHOOL OF SCALES

Provide each player with a pencil and lined paper. At the word GO, players are to write as many types of fish as they can think of in ten minutes. The one with the longest list wins. Suggested fish: goldfish, cod, sole, catfish, dogfish, snapper, salmon, trout, bass, yellowtail, gar, minnow.

CATFISH FREE-FOR-ALL

One player is chosen as the fisherman. He or she hides his or her eyes and counts to fifty, while the other players, the "catfish," hide. The fisherman tries to find the players and reach base ("shore") before the "catfish." To add to the confusion for the fisherman, the catfish may "meow" to one another. If a catfish is caught, he or she must become the fisherman.

TALL TALES

Players, one by one, try to outdo one another by telling the tallest fish tale. The winner is selected by the hostess (or host) and is awarded a cardboard placard, inscribed "First Prize Winner of Tall Tales."

PLACE CARDS

Make fishing poles of short sticks and string. Insert the sticks in holders and tie place cards to the free end of the string.

REFRESHMENTS

"Sea water" limeade, fish molds of lime jello with grapes for eyes; layer cake.

GHOST PARTY

by EILEEN M. HASSE

Halloween is an exciting time for a party. Make yours a ghost party with everyone dressed in white. The effect will be terribly spooky and so much fun. About two weeks before the party, write invitations on ghost white paper. Draw a pencil spook in the corner. Here is a jingle for your invitation:

Just any old gown or any old sheet
Will make your costume surely complete.
Come out for laughs or come just for scare,
Every ghost in the country is sure to be there.
Date: Oct. 31
Time: 8 P.M.
Place: (Your address.)

Before the party, clear a room to make playing games easier. Decorate the room with spooks made from paper bags. Blow up the paper bags. Tie them tightly with string long enough to dangle from the doorway or ceiling. Spray the bags with Christmas snow, or cover them with froth made by beating soap and warm water with a beater. With poster paints, make eyes and mouth. Then tape the spook heads to the doorway or ceiling.

When your guests arrive, greet them in your ghost costume. Under your sheet have a rubber glove filled with cold water. Twist a rubber band very tightly around the glove and fasten it to a short piece of broom stick or a ruler. Extend this hand for your guests to shake. There will be shrieks a-plenty.

Give each one a balloon in which you have slipped a strip of paper telling a fortune. The guest must blow up the balloon to find out what the fortune is. Your party is off to a bang!

A good game to play when everyone is there at last is **Pass the Pumpkin.** Have your guests stand in a circle. One guest is IT. You will have a whistle. The guests in the circle pass a small pumpkin to the right, behind their backs, while IT tries to guess who has the pumpkin. When you blow the whistle, the pumpkin is passed in the opposite direction. If IT guesses who has the pumpkin, IT takes the player's place in the circle. The player becomes the new IT.

Dead Ones is exciting to play. Pin a good-sized numeral to the back of each guest. One player, IT, goes from the room. The remaining players form a circle and march around the room until the leader calls two of the numbers. Then they stop marching, and those two numbers try to exchange places before IT rushes in from the other room, tagging one of the players—or both. A tagged player becomes a "dead one," and must stand in the middle of the circle until the last one is caught. If the game continues long, a new IT may be chosen by the leader. The last couple to be caught should be given a prize.

You will want to give a small prize to the best ghost at your party. Then you will be ready for refreshments.

Marshmallows toasted in the oven between soda crackers make tasty toast-ghostwiches. Serve them with tall glasses of Spook Cider, which is apple cider or apple juice with a sprinkling of cinnamon. Popcorn and apples are another good combination for a Ghost Party.

Just before your guests go home, give each of them a party favor. A candy lollipop draped with a square of white crepe paper or a white napkin can be used for a favor. Fasten the napkin or paper over the sucker, anchoring it with a rubber band. Let the paper flare out to cover the stick. Paste colored gummed dots for eyes and mouth.

Spook parties are great fun, especially if everyone is a ghost!

DOLPHIN DIP PARTY

by VIVIAN M. PRESTON

For younger junior highs

Lower the body heat on a hot, muggy July afternoon with a Dolphin Dip Party. A splashing good time can be had in a backyard pool, at a swimming club, lake, or river. Several tubs of ice-cold water with the help of a garden hose are always a possibility if there are no swimming areas around.

"Playful Dolphins" is the theme of the party. Keep your publicity posters and invitations consistent with the theme. Invitations could be made from heavy paper cut into the shape of dolphins. Guests can be divided into teams of dolphins and whales for the games.

WATER GAMES

Swim for a period of time. Then move into some planned activities.

Water Volleyball—A rope is strung across the middle of the pool. The group is divided into two teams. The game is played like regular volleyball. A volley is lost when the ball touches the surface of the water.

Relay Boat Race—Two players face each other on either side of the filled pool or tub of water in the yard, each with a toy boat provided by the hostess. Each player tries to get the boat to the other side by blowing it across the water. A suggested prize is a compass.

Fish Blow—A toy whale or any plastic fish or duck that floats may be used. All the toy boats from the preceding game are now in the water. Each guest tries to blow the whale or duck through the boats to the other side without knocking over a single boat. Each one who succeeds receives another prize, perhaps a package of Life Savers.

Bailing-Out Race—Place two buckets of water a few feet apart. Beside each pail have a quart fruit jar and a clam shell of equal size. The "dolphins" and "whales" line up for a relay in two lines. When a whistle blows, the leader of each line dashes to the bucket of water, dips the clam shell into it and transfers the water to the glass jar. The leader rushes back, touches the one at the head of the line, and goes to the rear. The team that gets the most water in the jar is declared winner.

The One That Got Away—Each guest is asked to describe the fish that got away while he or she was fishing. The one that gives the most detailed word-picture of the fish is the winner. A prize may be a fish hook.

"I Spy" Contest—Previous to the party the hostess could prepare "sails" of miniature marshmallows glued on white paper. These could be attached to bushes, trees, porch rail, etc. The one who sees the most sails is the winner.

Backyard Refreshments

At a backyard party, refreshments could be tuna fish salad, potato chips, assorted relishes. Ship Ahoy cookies (any plain cookie with appropriate frosting decorations: an anchor, fish, sailor hat, etc.), and seafoam. If a fire is permitted, you may want to roast wieners and toast marshmallows.

A HOLLY JOLLY

A Christmas Party for Younger Teens

by ERMA REYNOLDS

We're having a Holly Jolly
Filled with Yuletide fun and folly.
Please accept our invitation,
Be on hand with expectation.
Name . . . Place . . . Time

DECORATIONS

Huge holly wreaths made of green paper leaves, and red inflated balloons for berries, decorate the walls of the party rooms.

FUN

Holly Crown: The first guest to arrive is given a small holly wreath to wear, and is told this badge of honor can be worn as long as the person can avoid saying "no." Other guests try to trap the wreath-wearer into saying "no," and whoever succeeds gets to put on the wreath. If the party is large, have two or three wreaths in circulation. The person, or persons, wearing a holly wreath when the last guest arrives, win a prize.

Holly Pass: The guests are divided into two relay teams and sit facing each other. The leader of each team hangs a holly wreath over the toe of his or her left foot. At the starting signal, without aid of hands, the leader hangs the wreath over the left toe on the next player—and so on, down the line. If the wreath drops, it must go back to the leader and start down the line again. The first team to finish wins.

Holly Smash-down (a variation of musical chairs): Each player is given a paper plate, and a red and green crayon, and is instructed to make a holly wreath on the plate. When the work is finished, plates are displayed and the creator of the best-looking wreath is given a prize. Now the players form a circle and start marching, with their plate wreath held above their heads. At a signal they quickly put their wreath on the floor and sit on it. Last player to "smash down" is out

of the game. The contest continues until only one player remains.

Berry Scurry: Players line up in a row, and each one is given a large paper bag to put over his or her head as a blindfold. Raw cranberries, pinchhitting for holly berries, are scattered over the floor. At the starting signal, players put on their paper blindfold and get down on their hands and knees. In this position they scurry about trying to find the "berries." At the end of five minutes, the player with the most berries wins.

Holly Catch: Players form in couples. One of the pair is seated in a straight chair and holds an unsharpened pencil in his mouth. The partner, armed with a miniature holly wreath, stands six feet away and has three tries to land the wreath over the pencil. Partner in the chair can twist and turn his or her head, trying to catch the wreath. If the party is large, two or three couples can compete at the same time. Couples who succeed in landing a wreath are each rewarded with a prize.

Pic-a-Holly: Before the party, collect lots of used Christmas cards, making certain that many of the cards show holly in their design. Divide the players into two teams. At far side of room place two deep boxes, each containing a jumbled collection of Christmas cards, with an equal number of cards for each team. There must be as many holly-design cards in each box as there are players on the team. At the starting signal, leaders of each team put on a pair of huge mittens and run to their box where they fish around until they can find a holly card. Back they run with it to their team where player no. 2 takes the mittens and continues the relay in the same fashion. First team to finish is the winner.

WINTER FROLIC PARTY

by YVONNE L. SHAUL

Invite your friends for an evening of winter fun with invitations written on icicles cut from white art paper.

DECORATIONS

Use white balloons to decorate the windows. Hang the balloons in clusters. (See Icicle Parade Game to plan balloon clusters.)

A large snowman or two will also help with the decorations and later serve in the games.

An igloo made from large marshmallows may decorate the table as a centerpiece.

PLACE CARDS AND FAVORS

Wrap rectangular candy bars with soft centers in white paper. Use clear plastic tape to seal. Make "cracks" in these "icebergs" with black magic markers. Stick pennants (tiny triangles of paper glued to toothpicks) with the guests' names written on them into the bars.

GAMES

Big Thaw (Mixer)

To "thaw out" your guests, give each a number from the tray as he or she arrives. Tell them to find a paper in the room which has the same number and take it to the center. Here, the guests will place the papers together, in jig-saw fashion, to make a snowman.

When placing the pieces together, each guest will put his or her own initials on the piece with a GREEN marker.

The first person to find, place, and autograph his or her piece of the snowman rates a BLACK ICICLE (licorice stick).

Snowman Relay

Divide your guests into teams with blindfolds for each team and give each leader a red marker. Blindfold the leaders of both teams, turn them around after showing them the snowman (which has now been pinned to a wall) and start both players toward the snowman. The object of the game is for each player to write his or her own number on the same piece of the snowman which also has his or her autograph in GREEN crayon. Teammates may help by calling out HOT or COLD, but must not tell a player which way to go, or when to stop.

The team finishing first wins a prize, but the team placing the most numbers in the correct places wins the game.

Snow Talk

Before the party, prepare a tray of words which can be used to make sentences of not more than four words about SNOW. You can write out these sentences, such as SNOW IS FROZEN WATER . . . I LIKE DEEP SNOW . . . SLED RIDERS NEED SNOW . . . ALASKA HAS HEAVY SNOW, etc. These can then be cut into words, with the word SNOW discarded before placing them on the tray. (SNOW is the FREE WORD which all use in making SNOW TALK.)

The object of the game is to make sentences about SNOW. Several single words or duplicates of sentences should be included to provide sufficient material.

To play the game, seat the players facing each other, in rows. Pass a tray of words along each row, asking the players to take two words. When all have done so, the hostess will ask the first player on one team to use his or her two words, add SNOW and, if possible, say something about snow. If the player happened to draw WHITE and IS, he or she can say SNOW IS WHITE. But, if the words are YOU and HEAVY, he or she cannot make a sentence. Therefore he or she must wait until the second round to try again.

When the tray is passed for the second round, the players take only one word. This is done in the third round and all subsequent rounds.

If a player does not draw words for a sentence after the third round, he or she must return all the words to the tray and start over.

Whenever a player does make SNOW TALK, his or her team is given ten points and a goal of a given number of points decides who wins.

Toboggan Trip

Assemble a number of lightweight articles, such as sacks filled with paper, folded newspapers, sponges, foam-filled pillows, plastic bottles and other unbreakable and safe items, to load the toboggans quite high.

If the area is large, three teams can compete at one time, but two may be sufficient. Give each team a TOBOGGAN made from a large carton.

The object of the relay is to move "a pile of furniture" from one end of the room to the other without spilling. The relay begins when a signal is called. The players must load their toboggan with items from identical piles, each putting the same number of items on their toboggan. The teams start off with 100 points and lose five points each time an object falls off. (Fallen items are not returned to the toboggan.)

Icicle Parade

Inflate long white balloons, one for each guest. Make a list of ridiculous questions with laugh-provoking answers. Attach the questions to half the balloons for the boys, and tie the answer slips to the other half for the girls.

When the girls are asked the questions by the boys, they make no reply unless their slip answers the boys' questions. If this is a couple's party, the boy who asks a question which a girl answers becomes her partner for refreshments.

REFRESHMENTS

Borealis Soup: (Hot chocolate with tiny colored marshmallows floating on top)
Iceberg Pudding: (Neapolitan ice cream)
Avalanche Cake: (Plain white cake decorated with shredded coconut)

SECTION V
Additional Resources (All prices subject to change)

PROGRAM RESOURCES

The Art of Friendship. A short-term study unit. Student's book, 70¢. Teachers guide, 60¢. (Graded Press, United Methodist)

Babysitting. A seven-session course dealing with the fundamentals of babysitting. Student's workbook, 50¢; leader's guide, 75¢. (Christian Education Office, Reorganized Church of Jesus Christ of Latter Day Saints, P.O. Box 1059, The Auditorium, Independence, MO 64051.

The Bible and You. A readable, cartoon-style booklet that gives the basic facts about the Bible plus some tips on how to read the Bible. 25¢ each from Channing L. Bete Co., Inc., Greenfield, MA 01301.

The Fold-out Hang-up Push-out Global Think and Do Thing. A series of eight poster tabloids on current themes and Christian response for junior highs. Student's book, $3.00; teacher's guide, 75¢. (Division of Mission, United Church of Canada)

Getting Ready for Junior High School. A 16mm film in which a group of seventh graders discuss their fears and first experiences in entering junior high. 17 min., color. Rental $12.00 from BFA Educational Media, 2211 Michigan Ave., Santa Monica, CA 90404.

Generation Gap. A simulation game that deals with the interaction between youth and their parents. Four to ten players. $15.00 from Western Publishing Co., 1220 Mound Ave., Racine, WI 53404.

Gold Is the Way I Feel. 16mm film in which youth comment on their world. Useful for across-generation communication as well as for stimulating creativity in youth. Color, 9 min. Rental $10.00 from denominational film libraries. (Produced by United Methodist Communications.)

How to Go to School and Learn at the Same Time. George A. Chauncey, Jr. Media kit with 10 student books, 1 adult guide, 10 posters. Takes a close look at education and encourages student readers to do the same. Emphasis is on evaluation and then responsibility and action. $15.00. (John Knox Press)

I Am. In this 16mm film a young adolescent boy discovers that he is "somebody" by moving from a world of fantasy in which he assumes heroic roles to the real world where he discovers he doesn't have to be a hero to be important. Rental information from: Wombat Productions, Inc., 77 Tarrytown Road, White Plains, NY 10607.

It's My Decision As Long As It's What You Want. Open-ended discussion film dealing with parent-youth relationships. Mother and daughter try to communicate, but each feels the other is not being honest. 16mm, color, 13 min. (Produced by CRM Films, Del Mar, CA 92014)

People Who Help Others. Series of four filmstrips with recorded narration designed to help junior highs explore careers in which people "help others," such as day-care workers, physical therapist, community organizer. $37.50 with records; $45.50 with cassette. (Guidance Associates of Pleasantville, NY 10570)

Politics Is People. A study unit for junior highs that deals with political responsibility and encourages action. Packet $2.00; junior high guide, 50¢. (Christian Board, Disciples of Christ)

Thesis Mini Curriculum Cassettes. Malcolm Boyd with seventh graders talking about "Can God Really Help?" Guide included. $5.98. (Division of Mission, United Church of Canada)

Time Is My Own? A study unit for junior highs on the stewardship of leisure time. Folder with newspaper and variety of special resources. Packet, $2.00; junior high guide, 50¢. (Christian Board, Disciples of Christ)

Try the World Out. Camping resources for early teens. Leader's book, filmstrip, two records, student's book. $9.00. (Abingdon Press)

Understanding Your Parents. A two-part filmstrip with records that presents a variety of opinions regarding parent-child relationships from both points

140

of view through interview segments. $48.50 from Guidance Associates. Pleasantville, NY 10570.

What's Worth My Life? A study unit for junior highs that focuses on the values, commitments, and goals that persons have determined as worth their lives. Folder with newspaper and variety of special resources. Packet, $2.00; junior high guide, 50¢. (Christian Board, Disciples of Christ)

Weekend Pacs. Short study units for use during a weekend of study. Each pac contains a 32-page booklet and six leaflets providing material for eight hours of study for junior highs. Planning suggestions, session guides, worship helps. Packets are on: *Face Inward Outward; How Shall I Spend My Life?; Make Me a World; Really Living; Recreation: The Joy of Time; Shadows in Sunlight; Winners Keepers, Losers Weepers.* Each pac, $1.00. (Graded Press, United Methodist)

Leader Resources

Adolescence: Crisis or Opportunity. A film which deals with adolescent needs, especially in terms of finding identity. Interview with a psychologist, a YMCA counselor, and a high school teacher focus on the role of the adult in relating to adolescents. Rental $15.00 from Film Fair Communications, 10900 Ventura Boulevard, Studio City, CA 91604.

Audiovisual Idea Book for Churches by Mary and Andrew Jensen. A practical handbook describing how to use audiovisuals more effectively in the local congregation. $3.95. (Augsburg Publishing House)

Creative Activities in Church Education. Ideas for activities and helps for the leader in carrying them out. $4.00 plus postage and handling from Griggs Education Service, P.O. Box 362, Livermore, CA 94550.

Festival: A Mini-Course in Filmmaking by Lyman Coleman and Ken Curtis. A Serendipity book which uses three tracks to lead youth into a filmmaking experience: teambuilding, biblical research, making the film. $3.95 from Creative Resources (Word, Inc.), Box 1790, Waco, TX 76703.

Raise a Jubilee by Donald F. Jensen. General resources for people involved in planning an overall ministry with music for junior highs. $5.25. (Graded Press, United Methodist)

Retreat Handbook by Virgil and Lynn Nelson. Comprehensive handbook for planning retreats with many suggested program ideas for use with youth and adults. $5.95. (Valley Forge: Judson Press, 1976)

Vacation Time, Leisure Time, Any Time You Choose by Mary Calhoun. A book of program ideas and administration suggestions for vacation/leisure education for the whole church. $1.95. (Cooperative Publication Association)

SECTION VI
Index to EXPLORE,
Volumes 1 and 2

INDEX TO EXPLORE, VOLUMES 1 AND 2